Running on Empty

A story about three girls with eating disorders

by

Anna Paterson

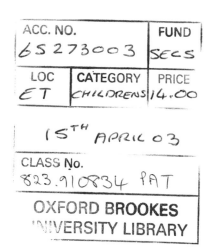
ISBN: 1 873942 94 X

Published by Lucky Duck Publishing Ltd.
3 Thorndale Mews, Clifton, Bristol BS8 2HX, UK

www.luckyduck.co.uk

Commissioned by George Robinson
Cover designed by Barbara Maines and Ben Robinson
Page layout designed by Helen Weller
Proofread by Mel Maines
Printed in the UK by The Book Factory, Mildmay Avenue, London N1 4RS

Dedications

I dedicate this book to Simon who as always has given me continuous support and help throughout its writing. Thank you also for being the best friend I've ever had.

I would also like to thank Mike Robeson for his constant help and encouragement. As ever, I couldn't have completed the book without you.

Biography

Running on Empty is Anna Paterson's third book. Her first book, *Anorexic* (Westworld International 2000) was an autobiographical account of her 14 year struggle with anorexia. Her second book *Diet of Despair* (Lucky Duck Publishing, 2002) was a self-help book on eating disorders for young people and their families. Anna is now recovered and spends her time trying to help other eating disorder sufferers who contact her daily. She works to raise awareness about the reality of these illnesses and is regularly asked to speak about her experiences. Anna is currently writing her fourth book. She lives with her fiancé Simon, who helps her with all aspects of her work including editing her books and they are currently saving up for their first house.

Contents

Part One

End of the Summer Term (Year 10)

1
Katee

"Useless! That's what you are! Totally useless! A waste of space!"

The words hit Katee like a slap in the face. She started to back away from her father into the furthest corner of the room. His anger was frightening as the words continued to race from his mouth, his face growing a deeper red with every passing minute.

"Why can't you be more like your brother? He's a success, but you – YOU ARE JUST A FAILURE!"

The tears started to trickle down Katee's face. She'd tried to hold them inside because she knew that any show of emotion angered her father even more. Moving further away from him, she found herself backed up against an armchair. Quietly, she climbed into it and tried to curl up into a tiny ball so that he would no longer notice her.

Seeing the tears in her eyes, her father started to shout even louder, waving his arms and her exam paper in the air. With one final mad flourish, he threw the neat pages of writing at his daughter and stormed out of the house.

Katee slowly breathed out but she felt no relief. He wouldn't be gone long. These days, he never left the house for any length of time. He had lost his job a few months earlier and with it his friends, although they hadn't really been friends. They were just work colleagues and their loyalty was to the company of Burton Computing, not to her father.

Sitting alone in the chair, she finally allowed the tears to flow unchecked. His words had hurt so much but he was right. She had received only 82% for her English exam. She was a failure. Her brother always received 90% or more for every test he took. His words echoed around her head – "A waste of space!" Yes that was what she was. A total waste of space. She wished she could just disappear. Why couldn't she ever make her father proud any more?

Brian Quinn had always been a workaholic. For most of her childhood he'd been a distant figure and even when he was at home, he spent more time with David, her brother. They shared the same interests and would spend hours together, playing computer games or watching sport. Katee knew that she wouldn't be included in these activities so instead would spend her free time with her mother.

Then, just a few short months ago, they'd heard the news that Burton Computing was struggling. Her father had always been a dependable worker but not outstanding and he had been upstaged by the young University graduates. He found himself receiving a very generous redundancy cheque and a firm farewell.

From that point on, everything had changed in Katee's life. At first, her father had tried to find a new job but time and again he was told that he was just too old. After a couple of months even the interviews started to dry up and it became obvious that he was not going to step into another job any time soon. Her mother became the only wage earner and increased her working hours whilst Katee took on many of the household tasks. Katee glanced at the clock and realised she'd been sitting and thinking for too long. She was already late putting the dinner on.

Grabbing a bag of potatoes, she started to count out the correct number for each person. Two for Mum, three for Dad, three for David and two for herself. As she reached into the sack for her second potato, she paused. She suddenly felt that she didn't deserve food like the rest of her family. She'd done badly in the exam and felt a need to punish herself. She decided to have one less potato that night. After all, they were her favourite part of the meal.

As she prepared the potatoes, Katee's mind started to wander. Words that her father had shouted at her during the last few months filled her head. "You're a lazy, ugly girl! I wish you weren't my daughter…Why can't you be clever like your brother?…You want more money for clothes? Have you grown out of your other ones? Putting on weight are you?"

A faint idea started to form in the back of her mind. What if she lost a little weight? The more she thought about it, the more it seemed like a good idea. After all, her Dad thought that she was fat and ugly. Maybe he would love her more if she were thinner. If she lost weight, she would also be smaller and less noticeable. He might not shout at her so much.

She finished peeling the potatoes and reached into the freezer, where she chose a large chicken pie for her parents and brother. She was vegetarian and had been for a year now – another reason why Dad picked on her. That day, instead of scrabbling further into the freezer for a vegetable burger for herself though, she started to build an elaborate salad on her plate instead.

With the potatoes, vegetables and pie cooking, Katee heard a key turning in the front door. She jumped with fright, as she knew it could only be one of three people. She prayed that it was her Mum or David and not her Dad back early.

"Katee! It's only me. Give us a hand with the shopping will you love?"

With relief, Katee scurried into the hall to help her mother with the bags. Distractedly, Jane Quinn handed a few of them to her daughter and shut the door behind her. She caught a brief glimpse of Katee's face and thought she noticed red-rimmed eyes.

"You alright love? You look like you've been crying," she called after her.

"No, I'm fine Mum. I've just peeled an onion and it made my eyes water. I have to do my homework now. The dinner's on and I'll be down in twenty minutes to serve up for you."

Katee felt a desperate need to protect her Mum and didn't want to talk about the earlier scene with her Dad. She felt too ashamed to repeat what he'd said because every word seemed to ring true. She was lazy and didn't work hard enough at school. 82% was a disgraceful mark and she really was a failure and a waste of space. Every day she was growing to hate herself just that little bit more.

Watching her daughter leave the room, Mrs. Quinn felt sad. She knew that Katee was growing up much too fast and had too many responsibilities already. After the school day ended she should be having fun with her friends, wandering around the mall looking at clothes and make-up instead of preparing family meals. Perhaps things would change when Brian found a job.

The key sounded in the lock again and a moment later, her husband walked into the kitchen. Jane looked at his face and sighed quietly. These days it just seemed to be permanently grey.

From the safety of her bedroom, Katee heard him return. A shudder ran through her body as she realised that she had become very afraid of her

Dad. She reached for her books and tried to settle down to her homework. Looking again at the now crumpled exam paper, she felt hopeless. She had let everyone down and her mind returned to the idea of losing weight. The exam paper swam before her eyes as her thoughts drifted away.

Maybe exercise would help her lose weight even faster.

Katee pushed her books to one side and after clearing a space on the floor, started to do sit-ups. By the time she reached her tenth one, she was in agony. Her stomach and back were aching painfully but she wasn't going to give up. She was determined to complete fifty before she had to go back downstairs and serve the dinner. Ignoring the pain, she continued to push herself harder. As she counted higher, each sit-up took longer. Her muscles ached and sweat was pouring off her face and body but she would not give up. Her father was always telling her that she was a quitter and this time she would prove him wrong.

Finally, Katee reached fifty sit-ups and allowed herself to stop. Her muscles were not used to this kind of exercise and she couldn't stop shaking. As she tried to stand, she had to reach out for a chair to balance herself. She sat on the bed and took some deep breaths to calm herself down. Her head was spinning and her heart racing but she felt a sense of achievement. She hadn't given up. She had completed her task. Grabbing a sheet of paper and a pen, she began to draw up her first exercise plan.

A knock on her door stopped her in her tracks. It was probably David wanting to borrow her Walkman again. But David never knocked on her door – he usually just walked in, chatting as he went. Katee looked up to find herself staring straight into her father's eyes. She quickly hid the exercise plan underneath her notebook and started to rise from the bed.

"Sorry Dad. I lost track of the time. I must serve up dinner."

"Why can't you ever do anything right Katee?" he sneered. "First the exam and now dinner. Get your head OUT of the clouds and join us in the real world OKAY?"

His voice rose with each word until he was shouting at her again. All the anger he felt about his life was suddenly flooding out onto his daughter. Not even able to look at her again, he turned on his heels and disappeared, slamming the door behind him.

Katee swallowed back her tears and hurriedly pulled on a sweatshirt before running down the stairs to serve up dinner. Cutting the pie and dividing the potatoes, she left her own plate until last. She added a pile of carrots, broccoli and beans to the colourful salad already arranged neatly on her plate. Finally, she slipped her single potato onto David's plate before handing out the meals. She then slid quietly into her seat in the corner and listened while David talked about the new sports team he had been chosen for that day. He was doing so well at school. It really was only her who seemed to be failing. With a deep sigh, she pushed away her half eaten plate of vegetables and salad. Her appetite had completely vanished.

2
Gemma

"I spoke with your French teacher yesterday and I was very disappointed with what she said". Gemma's mother, Clare Williams, looked across the table at her daughter who was nibbling on a piece of dry toast.

"She said that your grades were not as good this year so I think it may be time for you to start having extra lessons. You're nearly sixteen years old Gemma. Next year you'll be taking your GCSEs and you can't afford to fall behind."

With a deep sigh, Gemma nodded her head and took her plate over to the sink. Throwing away the remains of her breakfast, she could hear her mother still talking but the words were no longer registering in her head. Her mother seemed permanently disappointed with her this term. Nothing she did was ever good enough, whereas her mother was always such a success.

Mrs. Williams had just secured a promotion. Starting in September she'd be the new headteacher of Weatherbrook High School for Girls. This meant they were moving house during the summer holidays and Gemma was dreading the change of schools next term. She was certain that being the Headteacher's daughter was not going to be easy. Her mother would expect her to do well and set a good example to all the other girls at school. Gemma thought that her classmates would either tease or ignore her. Turning back to the table, she realised that her mother was still talking.

"I have to go in early this morning for a staff meeting. Can you do the washing up before you go please? And don't forget your lunch money I put it on the mantlepiece."

Gemma nodded and gave her mother a quick peck on the cheek before she hurried out of the kitchen, saying that she needed to pack her books for school. When she reached her room, Gemma shut the door and then pushed a chair against it. Her mother had a very annoying habit of just walking into the room without knocking. Reaching under the bed, Gemma pulled out two books. One was a diary and the other was a very well thumbed magazine entitled "Getting To Know Your Calories". Opening the diary, she wrote: "Three quarters of a slice of dry toast – 50 calories".

When she had finished writing, she shut the diary and started flicking through the calorie magazine. Her stomach rumbled painfully and she pressed her hand on it to try to stop the noise. Her breakfast hadn't been nearly enough to stop the hunger pangs but she felt determined. She was going to lose weight before she started at the new school. She desperately wanted her mother to feel proud of her, although she knew in her heart that she could never be as successful. A headteacher by the age of 42, her mother was slim, pretty and very intelligent. Gemma wanted to have just one of those qualities. Losing weight seemed the most achievable and that had prompted her to start dieting two weeks ago.

Hearing the front door slam and a car engine start, she knew her mother had left. She hid the books back under the mattress, grabbed her school bag and headed downstairs. Standing at the sink washing up the plates, Gemma's stomach grumbled loudly again and she started to feel a little dizzy. Maybe she should have some fruit before she left for school. She opened the fridge to look for the bowl of fresh fruit salad her Mum always had ready.

The fridge was quite full and the fruit bowl had been pushed to the back of the middle shelf. In front of it stood a magnificent chocolate cake that was smothered in thick, creamy icing and delicate chocolate flowers. Gemma's mouth began to water. It seemed so long since she had tasted chocolate and the smell was overwhelming. Gently pushing the cake to one side, she reached for the bowl of fruit that was hidden behind. As she reached over, her fingers brushed against one corner of the cake. As if burned, she quickly pulled out her hand and realised that her little finger was covered in chocolate cream. Instinctively she put her finger into her mouth to lick it clean. The taste was amazing and her mouth filled with an exquisite richness as all her taste buds came alive. Nothing in her whole life had ever tasted so delicious.

Before she even had time to think about what she was doing, she found herself reaching into the fridge for the cake. She grabbed a spoon from the kitchen drawer and started forcing huge mouthfuls of the chocolate cake into her mouth. Spoonful after spoonful was dug out of the large cake until Gemma could no longer even taste what she was eating. She didn't stop though. Sinking to the floor, she continued shovelling the cake into her mouth. Dropping the spoon at one point, she reached with her hands into the mess of cream, chocolate and sponge cake in front of her on the plate.

Gemma suddenly stopped and looked down at the floor. She cried out in disgust. Her hands were covered with the thick chocolate cream, her school skirt was stained and the chocolate cake had been reduced to a pile of crumbs and a smear of brown icing. Getting slowly to her feet, Gemma caught sight of herself in the mirror. Her face was also smeared brown with the chocolate and her hair had come loose from its ponytail. Tears started to roll down her face as she realised how many calories she had just eaten. A huge wave of guilt hit her and she felt really ashamed. Moving towards the sink, her stomach gurgled uncomfortably. She had been dieting for a while and her stomach was not used to rich food. An overwhelming feeling of nausea suddenly washed over her as she realised she was going to be sick. She rushed to the bathroom and made it just in time before she vomited violently.

Five minutes later, Gemma slowly stood up. Her legs were shaking and she could feel cold sweat running down her back. She carefully washed her face and rinsed out her mouth to try to get rid of the sour taste that was left. Looking in the bathroom mirror, she saw that her eyes were red and bloodshot from the crying and vomiting. Her face was now pale green in colour. She tidied herself as best she could and returned to her room to find a clean skirt. She would have to wash the stained one now or else her mother would wonder what had happened.

When she returned to the kitchen, she was horrified by the mess that greeted her. The whole floor was covered in small fragments of chocolate cake and one of the delicate flowers had been squashed into the lino. She put her skirt into the washing machine, started it going and began to frantically mop the kitchen floor. Within ten minutes the kitchen was clean and sparkling again but one problem still remained. Her mother would definitely notice that the chocolate cake was missing. Opening the dustbin, Gemma tried to search for a clue that might indicate where her mother had bought the cake. Hidden under a mound of potato peelings and leftover cottage pie, She finally found a discarded plastic bag from Grahams. Her heart sank. Grahams was the most expensive bakery in town. Her mother must have bought this cake for a special occasion and it was going to cost her a fortune to replace it.

She considered telling her mother that she had accidentally dropped the cake but what was the point in doing that? Her mother's face would just show that look of intense disappointment and the words "Oh Gemma, how could you?" would be heard yet again. She had no choice. She would have to use all her lunch money and most of her pocket money to replace the cake. She would also have to skip her first two classes if she was going to get to the bakery and back before her Mum arrived home for lunch. Grabbing her bag and the money she needed, Gemma took one last look around the kitchen to check for any telltale signs of what had happened and then hurried out the door.

3
Melissa

"Mel? Mel? Did you hear me? MEL!"

Melissa March snapped out of her daydream and looked up from her magazine. Her Mum was smiling at her across the breakfast table.

"Sorry Mum, I didn't catch what you just said."

"In another daydream were you Melly? You're an artistic one alright. I was just asking if you'd look after your brother this afternoon. I have to go to the hospital again."

"Sure Mum. No probs." Melissa smiled reassuringly at her Mum. "Are you having another check-up?"

"Yes, they just can't seem to get my insulin levels quite right at the moment."

Mrs. March had recently been diagnosed with diabetes and now spent quite a lot of time at the hospital. She had been told that her health problems were due to her size but although she was trying to diet, she wasn't losing much weight.

Melissa could not remember a time when her parents weren't overweight. She came from a happy home and her Mum and Dad usually seemed very cheerful. Food was everywhere though and Melissa grew up snacking on chocolates, crisps and cakes between large home cooked meals. Her Mum was forever saying: "Eat all your dinner Melly. You want to grow up healthy don't you?" Melissa always wanted to please, so she ate everything she was given and more.

Now at only 15, Melissa was already wearing large adult sizes. Buying clothes was tough and she felt so different to her friends who could choose from all the top fashion shops. Turning back to her magazine, she resumed her daydream. She stared at the tiny models and imagined what it must be like to be thin. Absentmindedly, she finished her thickly buttered toast and tried to force down her unhappy feelings. Everyone knew her as a joker – the cheerful clown who made everyone else smile. She couldn't look sad.

"I'll do the washing-up Mum," she announced suddenly. "You take it easy. Have you eaten the right amount of carbohydrates this morning?"

"Oh Melly, you are a wonderful daughter. Yes, I've been very good and had exactly what I need." Carrying her plates over to the sink, she gave her daughter a hug. "Well, I'll leave you to the washing-up while I get ready for work. Have a good day at school love."

A good day at school! That was a joke, Melissa thought to herself. Oh yes, people laughed and joked with her but only because she was always poking fun at herself. She had learned quite early on that people always teased the larger kids. From the age of six, other children had made fun of her size. It had hurt then and it still hurt now but she couldn't let people know that. She couldn't let them think she was upset by their cruel comments and horrible nicknames so she joined in with them instead. Soon she became the butt of everyone's jokes. The other children in her class loved good old Mel because she was so much fun but she knew they weren't true friends. Hardly anyone ever asked her to go clothes shopping or talked about boys with her and she was always left until last when teams were picked for games. Nobody ever wanted 'Massive March' on their team.

A lone tear ran down Melissa's face but she quickly brushed it away. She never let anyone know her real feelings. Her parents thought she was happy and to them she was a dream daughter. She was helpful around the house, worked hard at school and always seemed to be smiling. However, Melissa was actually very sad and just couldn't see a solution to her problems. She had tried to lose weight but it never seemed to work and she was beginning to feel hopeless.

She grabbed her school bag and yelled a goodbye to her Mum as she left the house. Putting on her Walkman, Melissa started listening to music and soon drifted into another dream. She was this wonderfully thin and attractive model who hung out in nightclubs with all the really cool pop stars. As if on autopilot, she entered the local newsagent and started collecting chocolate bars.

"Hello Melissa. How's your Mum today?"

Coming out of her daydream, Melissa smiled at the lady behind the counter.

"Hi Mrs. Clarke. Mum's okay thanks. She has another hospital appointment today but hopefully it won't be long before they can sort out her insulin."

"Oh that's good. She doesn't deserve to be having such a rotten time. She's such a sweet woman. Please give her my love. Okay, what have you here? Chocolate is it? That'll be 6 pounds 25 pence please."

Melissa handed over the money and hid the huge pile of chocolate bars at the bottom of her bag.

"Have a good day Melissa." Mrs. Clarke smiled warmly.

Melissa turned to wave as she left the shop and walked straight into the group of girls who were leaning against the shop front.

"Watch where you're going pudding face," yelled the girl Melissa had bumped into.

The shout was heard by everyone and all the girls in the crowd stopped chatting and turned to stare at Melissa. From the back of the group, a pretty young woman wearing a very tight skirt started to push her way to the front.

"Hey Mels! How ya doing?" she asked with a grin.

Melissa looked at the thin girl who was tottering towards her on huge platform shoes.

"Hey Caz. Yeah fine thanks."

"You just been in the shop Mels?" Caz continued.

"Erm…yeah," Melissa nervously answered.

"Whoa great!" Caz exclaimed. "Hey everyone…Smelly Melly here's been buying chocolate again."

In response, everyone in the crowd started to move closer to Melissa. She began backing up until she was crushed between the shop window and the group of girls.

"Hey give us some Jelly Belly," Cassie said in a baby voice. "Give wittle Cassie some yummy chocolate."

"Well I didn't actually buy any chocolate this morning Caz. I…I was just getting some gum."

The smile quickly faded from Cassie's face and was replaced by a spiteful sneer.

"I don't believe you greedy guts. You couldn't get through a day without your chocolate fix. You're addicted to it girl. Hand some over or else you'll regret it."

Melissa saw the change in Cassie and started to shake. Tears began to form behind her eyes but she fought them back and forced a cheery smile onto her face.

"I was just kidding you Caz. Of course I've got some chocolate. Hey… I am the chocolate queen aren't I? If I went on a diet, Cadbury's would go broke."

The angry look started to fade from Cassie's face and a look of greedy anticipation appeared. Reaching into her bag, Melissa pulled out the first bar her hand touched. She felt deep disappointment when she saw it was her favourite one but with a brave smile, she handed it over to Cassie.

"There you go Caz."

With tremendous relief, Melissa spotted their bus turning the corner.

"Hey look everyone…the bus."

All the girls started grabbing bags and searching for their passes. Pushing and shoving, they all shuffled forward. When the bus finally stopped, all the girls from the group raced up the stairs and forced their way to the back of the bus.

Melissa hung back from the group and watched them scuttle upstairs. Instead of following, she stayed downstairs and sat next to an elderly

woman whose face had a permanent smile due to her over
large dentures.

Slipping back into her world of sadness, Melissa started to think. She
had to lose weight. She just couldn't cope with the teasing any longer.
Tears felt close again as she thought back to the scene outside the
newsagents. She really hated herself. Why was she so weak? Why did she
eat so much? Why wasn't she pretty like the other girls? The pain she felt
was so intense that she reached into her bag for the only thing that she
knew would block it out. Food.

Part Two

Middle of the Autumn Term (Year 11)

4
First Meeting

The classroom was quiet while thirty girls worked on their test papers. Mrs. Hutchins looked up from her marking to check that everyone was busy. She smiled to herself when she saw the usual frowns on the faces of the girls who had been struggling that term. It was going to be tough to get everyone through the end of year exams but she liked a challenge and wasn't giving up on anyone yet. It was a shame they couldn't all be like Katee Quinn. She barely needed to be taught. She was always on time with her homework and never dropped below 90% in exams. Her eyes scanned the room until she found Katee sitting in the corner at the back.

A small doubt started to form in the back of her mind as she looked at her star pupil. Katee hadn't seemed particularly well recently. She had definitely lost weight in the last few months and now looked pale and tired. Mrs. Hutchins made a mental note to ask her if everything was alright.

Passing on round the class her gaze stopped at Gemma Williams. Now there was a puzzling girl. She had joined the school at the beginning of term and she still knew very little about her. Perhaps it didn't help that her mother was the headteacher. She seemed a very pleasant girl but never put herself forward in class. Probably just shy. Not like Melissa March, who was always joking and laughing with the other girls. She was a popular girl and seemed very well adjusted.

Mrs. Hutchins thoughts were interrupted as the school bell rang loudly.

"Stay in your seats please girls and wait until your papers are collected. As soon as your paper has been taken you can leave QUIETLY! Kim and Andrea? Will you start collecting the papers please?"

With a lot of scuffling and whispering, the test papers were collected and the girls started to file out of the room. Finally, carrying a large pile of papers and other books, Mrs. Hutchins followed her pupils into the corridor. The classroom wasn't left completely empty though. Three girls stayed behind. Katee, Gemma and Melissa.

After a lengthy pause, Gemma was the first to break the silence.

"I s'pose we ought to go to lunch. Does anyone want to join me?" she asked, walking over to Katee's desk.

Katee looked up slowly from the notebook she was writing in.

"I ate earlier and I just want some peace, so will you leave me alone?" she snapped.

Gemma was quite taken aback by the sharpness of Katee's reply. She hadn't spoken much with her before but certainly hadn't expected this reaction.

Backing away from the angry young girl, she turned hopefully to Melissa.

"Do you fancy some lunch Melissa?"

"Erm…thanks Gemma but I'd rather not. I'm on a diet. But I don't mind going for a walk with you to the corner shop maybe? I need some gum."

Gemma smiled. "Yeah, that would be great. I could do with the fresh air."

Katee looked up as the two girls left the classroom together and felt a wave of sadness. She was angry with herself. Why couldn't she have joined in? She would have loved to spend time with the other girls but once again, she had pushed people away. Her stomach rumbled painfully and she started to think about the food they could buy at the corner shop. Packets of cakes, chocolate bars and crisps started to dance in front of her eyes. They seemed so real that Katee felt she could just reach out and grab them. As she tried to imagine how the food might taste, her head was filled with an angry 'voice'.

"What do you think you're doing dreaming about food? You're not allowed to eat! You don't deserve food! You are FAT! FAT! FAT!!!"

All thoughts of food instantly vanished as Katee sat terrified and alone. After a while, she returned to her journal and began scribbling furiously…

October 21st

Had an exam in History today. Yuck! Don't know how I did. I tried really hard and revised for ages but still couldn't answer all the questions. I just can't concentrate any more. My mind keeps wandering. Dad is going to be so mad at me if I don't do well. He scares me so much. Last night I thought he was going to hit me. Saw Mrs. Hutchins staring at me during the exam. I bet she was thinking "What a fat, ugly pig that Katee Quinn is!" After the exam, Gemma Williams asked me and Melissa March to go to lunch. I said no and Gemma and Melissa left together. I wanted to go with them but I'm not allowed. I am FAT and disgusting and I don't deserve food like everyone else. I have to lose more weight. I have to be thin. If I can just be thin then maybe Dad will love me again.

5
Drawing Closer

Gemma and Melissa turned left out of the school gates and started to walk down the hill towards the corner shop. They walked in silence for a few minutes until Gemma started speaking.

"Katee seemed really angry today. Is she usually like that Melissa?"

"Oh please call me Mel. It's only my Dad and teachers that call me Melissa."

Gemma smiled. "Okay then. Mel it is. I bet people only use Melissa when they are mad at you huh?"

"Yeah, you're right there. And when Mum or Dad call me Melissa Alexandra March, I know I'm in really big trouble."

The two girls giggled together. When they'd calmed down, Melissa continued.

"Sorry Gemma, I didn't answer your question. It was about Katee right?"

"Yeah. I just wondered if she was always that…erm…well…kind of snooty and really angry."

"I can't really say that I know much about her," Melissa added after a moment's thought. "She really has kept herself to herself this term. Lunch times and breaks she always has her nose buried in that diary. I've seen people go up to her, just like you did today, and get the same kind of reaction. She just seems so mad with the world. I guess that puts people off because I don't think she has any close friends. She's really brainy and always comes top in every class but I guess that's about all I actually know."

"Wow. That's really interesting," Gemma said animatedly. "I thought I didn't know anything about her just because I was new. I had no idea that she was this real mystery figure. I tell you one thing I do know though. She is just so thin. Has she always been like that?"

"Oh geez Gemma, I really don't know. Sorry," Melissa replied awkwardly. "Erm…maybe. Hang on. Let me try and think back to last year."

An expression of deep concentration crossed Melissa's face and she stopped walking. Gemma patiently stood in silence next to her for a couple of minutes, until suddenly Melissa remembered.

"No she hasn't", she said excitedly. "I remember the school games at the end of the summer term. Katee had forgotten her games skirt and so she had to borrow one. The games teacher called out her size to the whole class, I would have died of shame if that had been me. Anyway, she was a size 14. To me that seemed so tiny and I would have killed to be that size. But I can still remember Cassie Jeffries yelling out something cruel like: "Miss, I have a spare skirt but…oh sorry…it's just a normal size 10, not a GIGANTIC size 14!""

"Urgh! What a bitchy comment," Gemma said, pulling a face.

"Yeah. Typical Cassie remark I'm afraid. All that girl ever seems to do is try and hurt people."

Gemma looked at Melissa and saw the intense anger on her face.

"You okay Mel?" she asked, concerned.

Shaking herself back to reality Melissa quickly responded. "Oh yeah, sorry. Erm…where was I?"

"Telling me about Katee's size…"

"Oh yeah. Anyway that was about it really. But I know she was a size 14 'cause Sam Trent had a sprained ankle that day and lent her the skirt. I know Sam is definitely a size 14 because I once went shopping with her."

"Well I'm telling you Mel…there's no way that Katee Quinn is a size 14 now. I'm size 12-ish right? And Katee's miles smaller than me. So that girl's lost loads of weight this year."

"Hmmm. That is a bit strange," Melissa said thoughtfully. "I guess maybe Cassie's comment could have made her think about starting a diet during the holidays."

"Yeah. Maybe," Gemma replied distractedly.

Gemma and Melissa turned the corner to enter the shop and bumped straight into Cassie Jeffries. As if by talking about her, they had made her appear.

"Ahhh Melly. Off to the shops to buy some more chocolate? And who's this with you? Little Miss 'My Mummy's The Headteacher' Williams." Cassie sneered at Gemma. "You're lucky I just finished my lunch Mels coz I'm not hungry right now but don't forget to save me some chocolate for later."

Pushing her way between the two girls, Cassie called out to her group of friends and started to walk back up the hill.

"That girl is truly revolting," Gemma said to Melissa as they entered the shop.

"Yeah…she isn't very nice is she? I guess I ought to get some chocolate though, in case she starts on at me later."

"What?" Gemma exclaimed. "You can't just give in to her demands like that Mel. That's bullying, you know? Do you give her chocolate often?"

"Oh it's not really bullying Gemma. I sort of let Caz think that she's a friend. The trouble is that I have to buy chocolate specially for her coz I'm on a diet."

Gemma felt puzzled by this last remark. She watched as Melissa grabbed ten bars of chocolate from the display and paid for them, before quickly shoving them into her large bag.

"You need that much chocolate for her?" she asked in astonishment.

"Oh no. I just thought I'd get some for my brother and Mum and Dad too, you know?"

"Right…" Gemma replied uncertainly.

Something didn't add up here. Either Cassie was forcing Melissa to give her huge amounts of chocolate or something else was going on. Gemma thought back to the ten chocolate bars in Melissa's bag and her mouth started to water. She shouldn't have allowed herself to go down to the store with Melissa. Once her mind was focused on chocolate, which was one of her 'bad' foods, she was in trouble. She knew that now she wouldn't be able to think about anything else until she'd had some.

Gemma could hear Melissa chatting away beside her. She smiled and nodded but her mind was elsewhere. She was already planning a binge, although she couldn't even admit to herself that she was doing it. The word 'binge' just seemed too horrible to even contemplate. It made her think of greed, lack of control and weakness and she didn't want to have any of those things. She wanted to be a success like her mother.

She tried to turn her mind away from chocolate but her thoughts kept returning to one of the bars Melissa had just bought. There had been a new kind that Gemma had never tried before and she was desperate to discover exactly what it was like. She had tried to read the label when Melissa was paying but could only make out the words 'caramel and rice'. She thought for a moment. She only had Art that afternoon and she could be late for that. No one would notice. Looking at her watch, she saw that it was only two minutes until the bell. She had to act quickly.

"Oh no Mel! I just remembered!" she said, raising her hands up to her face in mock horror. "Mum asked me to get her something and I didn't pick it up from the shop. I'm going to have to run back and buy it. Will you cover for me? Erm…can you tell Mr. Howard that I…erm…erm…?"

Gemma tried to clear her mind and think of an excuse.

"… that I had to go to the school nurse? I'll only be ten minutes. Please?"

"Oh…yeah sure Gemma. Be as quick as you can though."

Slightly confused by the sudden change in Gemma, Melissa continued up the hill. Her mind was full of so many different thoughts. She was trying to remember as much as she could about Katee Quinn and how she had behaved the year before. Thoughts about Cassie Jeffries also intermittently flashed in and out amongst confusing new feelings about Gemma. Had she just made a new friend?

Overriding all of these thoughts though was a strong desire to eat some of the chocolate she had just bought. Clashes with Cassie always left her feeling depressed and desperate to eat. Reaching into her bag, she pulled out a bar and tore at the wrapping. In two huge bites, the chocolate had disappeared and her tastebuds were bathed in an intense richness. She had to have more and grabbed the next bar that her hand touched. It was one of her favourites and tiny pieces of chocolate showered down her front as she forced huge chunks into her mouth. Within seconds, it had disappeared as well and she reached for a third. As she devoured large chunks of soft chewy toffee and rice, she heard a voice behind her.

"You'll be late for my class if you dawdle Melissa."

Melissa jumped so violently that she dropped her bag. Empty wrappers and chocolate bars fell out all over the pavement. As she tried to swallow the sticky caramel chocolate lumps in her mouth, Melissa dropped onto the floor and started shovelling everything back into her bag.

"Can I help Melissa? I didn't mean to make you jump," Mr. Howard said apologetically.

Finally able to speak, Melissa continued grabbing bars and wrappers. Unable to even look up at her Art teacher, she started to babble.

"No, no thank you Mr. Howard. I'm fine. Just a bit clumsy today. Been to the shop to buy lots of treats for my family. I really should be more careful. Sorry."

"That's okay Melissa. Um…you have some chocolate on your cheek just about…there," he carefully pointed out. "Why don't you pop along to the bathroom before class?"

Melissa's cheeks turned a deep red and the shame she felt was painful. It was bad enough that she'd been caught eating chocolate bars but by

Mr. Howard of all people. All the girls thought he was really cool and now he must think that she was just a revolting fat cow. She shuddered inwardly.

∞∞∞∞

Ten minutes later, as Melissa washed the tears and chocolate from her face, she began to make promises to herself again.

"I am going on a diet. This is it. The last chocolate I will ever eat."

Pulling the remaining chocolate from her bag, she headed for the waste bin. She would throw away the bars that tasted so nice but always made her feel so bad. Just before she reached the bin though she heard a noise. It was coming from the end cubicle. She first heard a scuffling and then a sound as if someone was being sick. Her own problems immediately forgotten, Melissa pushed the chocolate back into her bag and walked back down the row of identical cubicles.

"Is anyone there? Are you okay? Can I help?"

6
Feeling ashamed

Gemma watched Melissa continue up the hill. As soon as she saw her turn the corner towards the school, Gemma ran back to the newsagent. All she could think about was that new chocolate bar she had just seen. It was as if she was totally controlled by her feelings. Nothing else mattered. She had to have the chocolate that she craved so badly.

Gemma entered the corner shop and started grabbing packets of chocolate biscuits and thick bars of creamy chocolate. She didn't even stop to think of the price. She only knew that she needed that chocolate. Within seconds, her arms were cradling tempting packets of food and she went to the counter to pay. At the very last moment, she spotted a display with the new type of chocolate. She had to try that too so she reached out to take a couple of bars from the top of the pile.

As she leaned across the counter, one of the packets of biscuits slipped from her grip and as she tried to save the precious food, she lost her balance. Packets of biscuits and chocolate went everywhere and Gemma looked up to see the shopkeeper watching her.

"Well you've made quite a mess there. Do you really want all those biscuits or are you just trying to damage my stock?"

Blushing brightly, Gemma started grabbing the now broken biscuits.

"We're having a party at school and I was sent to buy the food. I'm really sorry I've made a mess."

Taking pity on her, the shopkeeper helped Gemma with the packets.

"Well I suppose it is good to see you girls enjoying yourselves a bit. I'm certain that school works you all too hard."

Smiling in response, Gemma paid the bill, left the store and started to run up the hill. She needed to find somewhere quiet where she would be alone. She headed for the basement toilets. They were always empty at this time of day. Locking herself in the last cubicle, she sat on the toilet seat and started to open her bag. She didn't even notice the antiseptic smell of cleaning fluid or the cloying stench of cheap soap. She was focused completely on her bag of food.

For five minutes she binged. Ripping open packets, she grabbed handfuls of chocolate and biscuits. The first few mouthfuls were blissful and she savoured the taste but the more she ate, the more she needed to eat. Like a starving animal, she gorged on the food. She ate faster and faster, barely tasting the sweet biscuits until all she had left was a bag of crumbs and some empty wrappers.

And then the guilt began.

What had she done?

The last time this happened, she had promised herself that she would never binge again. She had to get rid of the food she'd just eaten. Standing up, she turned around and forced herself to be sick. She hated doing this so much. She felt disgusting and ashamed but she had no choice. The first time she'd vomited after the chocolate cake, it had been an accident but since then she had learned how to make herself sick. Now every time she binged, she felt she had to vomit too.

Suddenly, she heard a voice.

"Is anyone there? Are you okay? Can I help?"

Gemma froze in terror. No one must ever know what she had just done. If they found out, she was sure they'd think she was vile. She kept very still, hoping that whoever was outside would eventually give up and go away.

"Hello?" The voice grew louder and more persistent. "Do you need help? Shall I get a teacher?"

When she heard those words Gemma knew that she had to leave the safety of the cubicle. If this girl brought a teacher down to the toilets then her secret would definitely be out. Hiding the bag of empty wrappers behind the toilet, she slowly opened the door.

"Gemma?"

"Melissa?"

They both announced each other's names at exactly the same moment.

"Are you okay Gemma? You look very green. Do you want to go to the sick bay and see the nurse?" Melissa asked with concern.

"No…it's okay Mel. I think I just have a bit of a bug. I'll be fine. Let's go to Art yeah?"

Melissa wasn't happy with her new friend's response. Gemma looked awful. Her eyes were bloodshot and her cheeks pale.

"Are you sure Gemma? You really don't look at all well."

After a great deal of persuasion, Gemma finally managed to convince Melissa that she would be fine. However, she had to promise that if she felt ill again, she would go and see the school nurse.

As they walked up the stairs to the art room, Melissa remembered what she had been thinking about on her way up the hill.

"Oh Gemma I meant to tell you. I remembered something else about Katee."

"Really? What was that?" Gemma asked with interest.

"Well it may be nothing but at the end of last term, just before we broke up for the holidays, she turned up at school with a really bruised face. Her eye was sort of black and she had a cut on her cheek. I remember Cassie pointing it out and asking her what had happened. Katee said that she'd walked into a door or cupboard or something and of course Cassie then started calling her 'clumsy klutzy Katee'. I guess that was why I remembered it so clearly. I really hate it when Cassie turns on people like that."

"So what are you saying Mel? Do you think someone hit Katee?"

"Oh no. Well...no, I don't think so. But I wondered if she was maybe ill. I've read about these illnesses where you bruise easily. And thinking back, I remembered seeing Katee with quite a few bruises."

Gemma was very quiet for a while. This was interesting but very worrying information. Her own problems were totally forgotten as she started to think about the angry young girl who always looked so lost and alone. Maybe she should try talking to Katee again? Even if she received the same angry reaction, at least she would have tried to help. Gemma understood what it was like to feel alone and unwanted. Maybe Katee just needed a friend.

7
Eating Out

Katee swung open the garden gate and was surprised to see lights on in the house. Her mother had warned her that morning that no one would be home after school and had asked her to start the dinner as usual. Cooking was something Katee loved doing these days. Since she'd started her diet, food had become very important to her. Preparing and cooking meals was comforting. Watching her family eat and enjoy the new dishes she prepared was the most exciting part of her day.

There was one major problem though. The more weight she lost, the more suspicious her mother became. A few months ago, it had been easy to excuse herself from meals. She would take a plate of food upstairs with her, pretending to her Mum that she had lots of homework to do. As time passed though and she became thinner, Katee's Mum grew more insistent. She wanted to see her daughter eat with the rest of the family.

Katee started to become very devious as a result. Previously she had been such an honest young girl, always truthful and open with her parents. Now she was a closed book. She definitely couldn't talk with her Dad. He had hurt her too much. And although she trusted her Mum a little more, she couldn't tell her about the diet. What if she made her eat properly? She couldn't bear the thought of having to eat more food again. Even though she was hungry and desperately craved the tastes she used to enjoy, eating still felt very wrong. She wasn't thin enough yet. She just had to lose a few more pounds.

Pushing open the front door, Katee was greeted by the sound of her parents laughing. This was something she hadn't heard in months. She walked into the kitchen and saw her parents waltzing around the room. When he spotted his daughter, Brian broke off from the dance and rushed over to grab Katee. Lifting her up, he spun her around as he used to do when she was a child.

Amazed, Katee stared at both her parents.

"Has something happened?" she asked.

"Your father got a new job today honey," her mother announced happily.

"Starting Monday, I am officially a member of the work force," Brian continued. "I'll be earning enough money to keep this family running smoothly again."

Katee felt a huge wave of relief wash over her. If her Dad was working again, then her life would be so much better. His anger and mood swings had all been due to his unemployment. Suddenly everything was going to be okay again.

"To celebrate, we're all going out for a special meal," Jane Quinn announced.

The feelings of happiness that had just washed over Katee instantly evaporated. She couldn't go out for a meal with her parents. How would she avoid food? She couldn't eat high calorie restaurant food. She'd become gigantic overnight if she did that. Somehow she just had to get out of this meal.

"Erm…that's a really nice idea Mum but I wasn't very well at school today and I don't think I should come," she muttered.

Her father's expression immediately changed. The cheerful smile that had greeted her only minutes earlier was now replaced with a deep frown and he began to shout.

"Do you know how selfish and ungrateful you are? You will come with us to the restaurant. This is my special evening and for once young lady you're going to make an effort to be a part of this family. Don't think we haven't noticed you disappearing upstairs every chance you get. Ashamed of your Dad were you? Ashamed to sit down at the table with an unemployed man? Well I've got a job now and you can damn well celebrate with me."

Katee felt tears prick the back of her eyes again. Why was Dad still so angry? He had a job now. He should be happy and cheerful. Jane could see the distress in her daughter's face and tried to gently soothe the situation.

"Come on love. It'll be fun. It's only going to be the four of us having a nice quiet dinner. If you don't feel well at the restaurant then you can have a lighter meal but we'd love you to come."

Katee knew that her mother was only trying to help but part of her felt betrayed. Why did her Mum never stand up for her? She'd heard how Dad had just yelled but she hadn't said a thing. In fact she was backing him up. Maybe she was a little scared of him too? Katee knew that her mother always tried to appease people. She didn't like conflict in the family and would do almost anything to keep her husband happy.

"Why don't you go upstairs and change love?" Jane said softly. "Put on something pretty. This is a celebration. Our lives are going to be so much better from now on."

Katee turned and quietly walked away. What was she going to do? She had to work out a plan. Opening the top drawer of her bedside cabinet, she dug around under her socks until she could feel a book. This was her calorie book and it had become her bible over the last few months. Katee now knew the calorific value of every food available. She didn't actually need to look anything up any more but whenever she was stressed, she turned to the book for comfort and reassurance. Reading through the section called "Eating Out", her heart sank. Everything just seemed so high in calories. Even most of the salads contained more calories than she ate in a whole day.

"Katee are you ready yet? We're going to leave soon."

Her mother's voice was insistent and Katee knew she had no choice but to go with the rest of her family. Opening her wardrobe, she reached for her favourite jeans and shirt. The jeans were huge on her now but she had found a belt that kept them up. Slipping another shirt over the top of the jumper she was wearing, Katee made her way back downstairs.

"Is that what you're wearing?" Her father sounded disgusted.

"Yeah Dad. It's my favourite."

"Well you look like a boy. Can't you ever do anything right! Why couldn't you look pretty for once, instead of bundling yourself up like some arctic explorer? I really do despair of you."

Hanging her head in shame, Katee made her way to the car. Why did she even bother to try? Her father hated her. It was just so obvious now. She had thought he was being cruel to her just because he'd lost his job but that couldn't be true any longer. Why was he still being so horrible to her now when he should be happy? It must be her. She must deserve this treatment. She really was a terrible person who was always wrong. She decided she would have to punish herself as soon as they returned from the restaurant.

8
Making bargains

"Katee are you awake? If you don't get up now you'll be late for school." Jane's voice echoed up the stairs.

Katee sat up in her bed and pushed back the covers. Last night had been one of the longest of her life and yet she still hadn't wanted the morning to come. Her eyes hurt from crying and lack of sleep. Her body felt weak and bruised, as if she'd been hit by a truck and she was numbed by her mixed emotions.

The meal at the restaurant had been a complete disaster. The menu had boasted a huge array of wonderful delicacies, all of which seemed to contain butter, sugar or cream. Katee stared at the list of dishes glassy eyed. The more she looked, the worse her panic became and the angrier her father grew. In the end, seeing her daughter's distress, Mrs. Quinn chose a plate of Linguini pasta for Katee.

Filled with terror and panic, Katee started to feel a rising anger. How dare her mother choose her such a fattening dish? What right did she have to make such a decision? She wasn't a child any more and she wasn't going to be treated like one. In a rare show of strength, Katee stood up to her parents.

"I won't eat this meal! I feel sick and I'm going to sit in the car."

Her comments only fuelled her father's already volatile temper though and his harsh words cut straight through the friendly noises of the busy restaurant.

"You spoilt little brat! You will sit down and eat every mouthful of your meal or you'll wish you hadn't been born!"

Heads started to turn and other diners stopped eating as they tried to discover what all the fuss was about. At that moment, a waitress appeared with plates heaped full of food and the Quinns all fell silent. Katee stared wide-eyed at the size of the dish placed before her.

She felt consumed by feelings of frustration and hurt. Right then she hated her father more than ever before. Digging her fork into the huge pile of food in front of her, she forced herself to eat just a tiny amount of the pasta. The delicious taste of creamy mushroom and garlic set her tastebuds tingling. She tried to remember how long it had been since she had tasted proper food. For months now, she had lived on the lowest calorie options available. Tiny slices of dry diet bread that tasted like cardboard. Crackers that had no flavour but which had to be eaten to calm just a few of her ravaging hunger pains.

The wonderful taste of the pasta sent Katee into another panic. The 'voice' in her head always told her that she wasn't allowed to enjoy food. She had to obey that 'voice' or else she would gain weight and become fat again. What should she do? As if on cue, the tormenting words began to echo around her head.

"What are you doing eating that food? Do you know how many calories that pasta contains? If you eat all that, you'll be massive by the morning."

Katee started to silently talk back to the 'voice' in her head as if it were completely real.

"I have to eat this food or else I don't know what my Dad will do. He'll probably throw me out of the house and then where will I go? I promise I'll exercise all night if I have to and…and…and I won't eat anything for the next four days. I promise."

Although she didn't realise it, Katee had begun to make bargains with the 'voice'. Bargains that were dangerous and which could ruin her life. She didn't even realise that she was ill. All that mattered was losing weight and pleasing the 'voice' that was now whispering persistently in her head.

"Katee, stop picking at the meal and eat it properly!"

Her father's sharp words brought her quickly back to reality. She grabbed her fork and angrily started shovelling huge mouthfuls of the dripping pasta into her mouth. If her father wanted to make her sick, then she'd be sick. Ignoring the 'voice' in her head that had started to yell, she continued to attack her meal. The more she ate, the sicker she felt. Her stomach wasn't used to food of any kind and the rich heavy pasta sauce was too much. Halfway through her meal, she had to stop.

"I'm sorry but I really can't eat any more. Sorry Mum. Sorry Dad. I tried."

Speaking quickly before her husband became angry again, Jane Quinn gently took charge.

"You did very well Katee. It's lovely to see you enjoying your food again. Let it settle for a bit and then we'll all have some dessert."

The words were spoken with kindness but the guilt Katee suddenly felt was tremendous. Her Mum was right. She had eaten such a lot. She'd undone all the hard work of the last few months. She could already feel her weight rising as she sat in the restaurant. She had to stop the weight gain. She had to think of a solution. Suddenly she had an idea and she turned to her Mum.

"Would it be okay if I went outside for a bit of fresh air before dessert? I'll only be a few minutes."

Jane looked at her husband to gauge his reaction. The meal had seemed to calm him and he was happily chatting to David about the latest football scores.

"Sure love but don't be long. We want to celebrate your father's new job with a very special dessert."

Katee slipped out of her seat and raced for the door before her father could notice that she was leaving. The sharp Autumn air felt bracing after the over-heated restaurant. Looking up and down the street, Katee was pleased to see that it was empty. She started to run as fast as she could down the road. She had to burn off some of the calories before they turned into fat. Exercise was the only solution. As she reached a crossroads, she remembered that the restaurant was part of a small block. If she ran really fast, she could make her way round it before she had to go back in for dessert.

As she ran, all she could think about was the pasta in her stomach. The faster she ran, the sicker she felt but she couldn't stop. This was the only chance she had to burn up some calories. All too soon, she arrived back at the restaurant and had to force herself to return to her family. Her mother looked up as she slipped into her seat.

"Are you okay Katee? You looked flushed."

"Yeah Mum I'm fine. It's just cold outside."

She realised that the exercise had left her hot and sweaty, and she needed to deflect the attention away from herself before her father noticed. Thinking fast, she grabbed the menu.

"Has anyone ordered dessert yet? The ice cream looks really good."

A heated discussion began over the desserts and Katee felt relieved that her parents were no longer looking at her. When it finally arrived, Katee's fear returned and the panic she felt was unbearable. She forced herself to eat a little of the decorative dessert, knowing that her night would be spent doing hundreds of exercises.

With the meal finally over, Katee stood up. Her Dad was smiling at her and forgetting how angry she was with him, she automatically smiled back. He put an arm around her shoulders and pulled her towards him. His words then filled her with dread.

"Well that was nice wasn't it Pumpkin? We really must do this more often. Family meals out are so much fun and now that I'm working again, we don't have to worry about saving money. We'll make it a regular treat."

Katee heard the 'voice' in her head start to speak.

"You're going to have to get out of those 'treats' you know? If you go out for a meal like this every week, you'll be the Queen of Blubber. Your thighs will expand until you burst out of your jeans. FAT! FAT! FAT! That's what you'll become!"

The 'voice' continued to torment Katee on the short drive home and as soon as they arrived back at the house, she raced upstairs and locked her bedroom door.

The exercising began immediately and continued for hours. Before long, her muscles started to burn and her joints ached. She felt a tightness in her chest and her breathing became more difficult but she forced herself to continue. All she could think about was that meal and the hundreds of calories she had eaten.

Finally, at three in the morning, Katee collapsed in a heap. She just couldn't continue any longer. She was beaten. Crawling into her bed, she hugged her old battered teddy bear and fell into a disturbed sleep that was filled with nightmares about huge plates of food.

"Katee did you hear me?" Her mother's voice was louder and more insistent this time.

Snapping out of her dream, Katee called out in reply to her Mum. She quickly pulled on her school clothes and packed up her books. Her muscles ached painfully from the exercising and she found it hard to walk properly. She knew that she really couldn't face seeing either of her parents that morning. When she heard them in the kitchen, Katee slipped down the stairs and out the front door, yelling a quick goodbye as she went.

Slowly she walked to school, trying to work out just how many calories she had burned off the night before with all her exercising. Suddenly, from behind, she heard a light thumping that was gradually getting louder. A minute later a voice called out her name.

"Katee? Katee? It's me. Gemma Williams. Can I walk with you?"

With a puzzled look, Katee stopped and turned around. Annoyed that her peace had been disturbed yet again, she frowned deeply. What was this girl's problem? Wouldn't she ever leave her alone?

9
Home Worries

"Mum, I really think I should stay home today. I want to be here in case there's any news about Dad."

"I understand that Melly but there's really nothing you can do here. We need to try and carry on as normal. Moping about the house won't help your Dad."

"But Mum, I just won't be able to concentrate at school," Melissa whined.

"You'll get by. I think it'd be much better for you to be with your friends. Here's some money. I didn't have time to make you any lunch. Now go on…GO or else you'll be late."

"Okay but you promise to let me know if you hear anything?"

Melissa took the money, collected her schoolbooks and left the house. She felt tired and drained after the trauma of the previous night and school was the last place she wanted to go. She was still trying to come to terms with what had happened and she wanted some time and space to think. Her Dad had always seemed so healthy. If anyone was going to get sick, she thought it would have been her Mum. Sure Dad was overweight but so were all her family and they were fine.

Her father had started experiencing chest pains at work the day before. He'd just assumed he had a little indigestion and had started taking antacids. The pain didn't ease though and by the time he arrived home, he was sweating and having trouble catching his breath. Melissa thought back to her mother's reaction and was very proud of the calm, responsible way she'd dealt with the frightening situation. It was all too easy to panic when you felt afraid but her Mum had seemed totally in control. Realising that her husband needed a doctor very quickly, Mrs. March had phoned for an ambulance immediately.

Within ten minutes, Melissa had watched two paramedics carefully stretcher her father into an ambulance. She had wanted to travel with her mother and father to the hospital but someone had to look after her younger brother. The next two hours had been terrifying. She had tried not to seem at all worried for the sake of James. He was only six years old and she didn't want to frighten him.

Although she carried out the normal routine of getting dinner and sitting down to watch the soaps, nothing felt right. What was happening at the hospital? Had her Dad's condition got worse? Was it a good or a bad sign that she hadn't heard anything?

At eight o 'clock, the shrill ring of the telephone made her jump in surprise. She grabbed the receiver and listened intently to her mother's voice.

"Hello Melly love. Good news. Your father's out of danger. They want to keep him in for a few days though to check him out properly. They think it could have been a very minor heart attack so it's important that he stays in the hospital for a while. They did say he had to lose some weight though. You should have seen his face when they told him 'No more chips'. I'm sure he was more upset by that comment than anything else this evening."

Melissa let out a deep sigh.

"That's such a relief Mum. I was imagining the most terrible things and was certain he was going to die. Yeah, we'll have to sort out his diet. He's going to have to stop eating chocolate too. Do you know he has a secret drawer full of it in his workshop? I found it the other day when I was looking for my stapler."

Mrs. March giggled lightly.

"Oh yes, I've known about your father's drawer for a number of years. Where do you think I used to go for chocolate when it was my time of the month? Those chocolate cravings used to get me every time. He never mentioned that any was missing though. You see the secret chocolate buying would've had to stop if he'd confronted me about it. I wish I'd talked to him though. I feel guilty that I didn't take more care of his diet. Oh well, things will certainly have to change now... Melissa?...Melissa? Are you still there?"

As Mrs. March chatted about her husband and his secret chocolate buying, Melissa's mind drifted back to the previous afternoon at school. Her cheeks blushed again as she remembered being caught gorging on chocolate bars by Mr. Howard.

"Sorry Mum. Yeah I'm still here. I was just thinking that we should all go on a diet with Dad. How about a family competition with a prize each week for the person who loses the most weight?"

"Oh I don't know Melly. You know how important it is to me that you kids have a healthy attitude to food. Dieting can cause problems for the rest of your life."

Melissa certainly did know about the problems of dieting but this idea was too important to her to drop.

"But Mum listen to me. Dad needs some motivation. We have to make this fun for him or else he's going to be a nightmare to live with. How about if he also starts collecting the money he would have spent on chocolate? It won't be long before he can treat himself to something really nice."

Melissa's mother was, as always, impressed by her daughter's kind heart. She always wanted to help and offered endless suggestions to whoever was struggling.

"I'll pass on those thoughts to your Dad love. Now let me say goodnight to James and then he can pop off to bed. I'll be home in about an hour. They're moving your Dad onto a ward in a few minutes, so I'll see him settled for the night before I leave."

"Okay Mum. You take care and I'll see you soon."

The rest of the evening hadn't been too bad but Melissa still felt worried about her Dad. Heart attacks really frightened her. She hated it when they showed them on hospital programmes or documentaries. She'd always wanted to be a nurse but lately her growing fear of medical problems meant that she wasn't so sure any more. She felt ashamed that she was nervous about visiting her Dad in the hospital. What if he had lots of tubes and machines around him monitoring his heart? Melissa gave a shudder. Maybe she would be needed to look after James again and wouldn't have to go.

Pushing the thoughts of hospital and the night before to the back of her mind, Melissa realised that she was late for school. She started to hurry and reached the school gates just as Cassie Jeffries appeared with her gaggle of identically dressed friends. Melissa was filled with disappointment. It was too much to hope that she would be gentle for once. Melissa just didn't have the strength to deal with her today. Cassie's high-pitched voice rang out across the emptying playground.

"Ahhhhh…look who it isn't. Hey there Marchers! Whoa, you look really hot and sweaty. Been jogging? Trying to lose some weight are you? Maybe you should come to my aerobics class. I'm sure my teacher would love the challenge."

Angry and fed-up, Melissa had finally run out of patience.

"Look Caz, just leave me alone today okay? My Dad's in the hospital with heart problems and I just don't need to hear any of your sly little digs. Why don't you just go and play with your make up okay?"

No one had expected such an outburst from Melissa March and the shock showed on Cassie's face. A couple of nervous giggles were heard from among her group of friends but Melissa didn't hang around to wait for a reply. She knew that she would pay for her boldness later but right now she felt good. Standing up to Cassie Jeffries was not an easy task but it actually hadn't been nearly as bad as she thought it would be.

She found her locker key and made her way to the basement, where she had her second surprise of the morning.

Standing by the water fountain were Gemma Williams and Katee Quinn. And Katee was actually giggling.

10
Catching Up

Gemma could see Katee walking ahead of her and realised that this was her chance to try again. She knew it wasn't going to be easy to chat to her but she wasn't ready to give up yet. She started to walk faster and at the same time called out.

"Katee? Katee? It's me. Gemma Williams. Can I walk with you?"

Gemma ignored the look of annoyance and disappointment on Katee's face and started talking at a fast and furious pace.

"Hi. I've never really had a chance to introduce myself properly. I know we're in a lot of classes together and obviously we have the same tutor group…but I guess it's not always easy being new and I've sort of kept myself to myself. I hope you don't mind me saying anything but you seem to do the same…I see you sitting in the classroom at lunch time and writing a lot. Do you wanna be a writer when you leave school… or maybe a journalist?"

Realising that she had been talking non-stop, Gemma came to a sudden halt. She was certain that Katee would think she was a complete idiot and choose to just ignore her. She looked up nervously and was amazed to see that Katee was actually smiling. Encouraged by this reaction, Gemma started chatting again.

"I'm sorry, I think I may have babbled a bit then. I do that when I'm a bit nervous you know? Not that I'm nervous about talking to you. It's just… well it's just… I think I'd like to get to know you a bit better. I haven't really made any friends since I got here. It's not easy being the daughter of the headteacher you know? Everybody treats you kind of…funny. And of course joining the school late means everyone already has friends and well… well it's just a bit difficult you know?"

Gemma ground to a halt again. She never usually talked about her own worries. She really did try to keep herself to herself because over the years she had found that trusting people didn't usually work out. The number of people who'd hurt her in the past had left her feeling nervous about being honest. She had actually surprised herself by being so open with Katee.

Katee's thoughts were racing too. She knew that she shouldn't let Gemma get too close. The 'voice' in her head told her not to trust anyone but she just felt so lonely. She desperately wanted a friend. Someone she could chat to during lesson breaks. Someone she could spend time with at the weekend. Someone she could even share her thoughts with.

Gemma was just about to speak again when Katee finally began to talk quietly.

"I…I can understand that it must be…difficult for you Gemma. I know what it's like to erm… to… um… well yeah anyway…"

Although her reply was short, Gemma sensed a deep understanding in Katee. Had she been bullied herself perhaps? She knew that Cassie had teased her about her weight during that games lesson but had other things happened as well? She was desperate to know but realised that she had to go very slowly. The image of a rabbit frozen in the headlights of a oncoming car filled Gemma's head. Katee seemed so fragile and Gemma knew that if she pushed her too hard to talk then she would just run away. She thought it might be wise to move onto safer subjects until she had Katee's complete trust.

"What lesson have you got first Katee? I have double Maths. I hate that subject soooo much. I just can't get the hang of Algebra."

"Oh yeah…I know. But it's not actually as bad as it seems. I've worked out a special trick that makes Algebra really simple. If you'd like…I could maybe show it to you?"

Katee came to the end of her sentence and immediately wished she hadn't opened her mouth. Gemma was going to think that she was such a nerd. Who worked out special maths tricks in their spare time? How dorky was that?

"Hey, that would be brilliant!" Gemma said enthusiastically and then sniggered loudly. "Miss Evans will pass out if I can suddenly do Algebra properly."

Katee started to giggle with Gemma. Miss Evans was quite an old-fashioned teacher. She wore old ladies dresses even though she was only in her late thirties and always had her hair tied up into a tight bun. All that seemed to matter to her was Maths and she became very agitated if a student couldn't understand a concept. Miss Evans had been focusing on Algebra for weeks now but Gemma just couldn't get the hang of it.

As they laughed together by the water fountain, Gemma spotted Melissa walking towards the lockers and she called out.

"Mel! Over here! Come and join us?"

Melissa felt a little buzz of happiness when she heard the words. It had been a while since anyone had called out to her like a friend. She walked excitedly over to the two girls but was disappointed to notice that Katee seemed to become nervous and fidgety when she joined them.

Almost immediately, Katee spoke up.

"I…I have to go to the toilet before class Gemma, so…I'd better go. See you later."

"Okay Katee. See you later," Gemma replied, slightly confused by Katee's sudden change of mood.

Melissa felt sad. She was sure that she had walked in where she wasn't welcome and immediately started to apologise.

"Gemma, I'm really sorry. I obviously interrupted and made Katee feel awkward. I was so amazed when I saw her giggling with you but I feel really bad now. I can't seem to do much right at the moment."

"Hey Mel, don't be so hard on yourself. You know that Katee's like a…" Gemma remembered the image she'd pictured earlier. "…like a frightened rabbit. I know it's going to take me a while to get her to trust me but I really think I should carrying on trying. This morning, I got the feeling that there's something very wrong which she isn't talking about. Maybe bullying or something. I don't know what exactly but I want to try and help. When you get past her prickly outer shell, she seems really cool. Anyway, I'm babbling again – something I've done all morning. How are you Mel? You look kind of tired."

Melissa explained her Dad's condition to Gemma and started to feel a sense of relief as she shared her fears and worries. She finished her story by talking about the incident with Cassie, just as the girl in question stomped past them on the way to her locker. Without her friends, Cassie seemed much less intimidating and even quite pathetic. Melissa couldn't really understand why she often felt so nervous around this silly little girl.

Together, Gemma and Melissa collected their books and made their way to the classroom. As they walked down the corridor, they noticed a large crowd was gathering outside their classroom door. Hurrying forward, Melissa tried to balance on her toes to look over the heads of the other students. She was unable to see anything and so turned to the girl on her right.

"Do you know what happened? Is everything alright?" she asked, concerned.

"Well I only just got here myself," the girl replied. "But they're saying that Katee Quinn just collapsed. Fainted I think. Someone's just gone to get the nurse."

11
Discovered

Gemma and Melissa looked at each other in complete disbelief before Melissa finally began to speak.

"What's going on Gemma? Katee was fine just a couple of minutes ago. This is so weird. Maybe that girl got it wrong."

Gemma didn't want to worry Melissa but she was starting to have an idea about Katee's problem. She was piecing together the jigsaw puzzle and the picture that was emerging was not a good one. She was still a little unsure about her thoughts though and didn't want to worry Melissa unnecessarily. She needed more information.

They heard the nurse arrive and saw a middle aged woman start to push her way forward.

"Will you please let me through? Don't crowd the girl for goodness sake. She needs some space and fresh air. Come on. Move aside. There's nothing to see. Go back to your classes."

The sharp voice of the school nurse cut through the crowd and all the girls started to disperse. Within a couple of minutes, Gemma and Melissa found themselves alone with just the nurse. They both gasped in shock when they saw Katee on the floor. Her skin was so pale and translucent that she almost looked dead. She barely seemed to be breathing and Gemma felt a need to touch her to check she was still alive. As she reached out, she heard the sharp voice again.

"What are you doing? Shouldn't you be in your class?"

Gemma quietly started to explain.

"Katee's our friend and we just wanted to check that she's alright. Is she going to be okay?"

The nurse started to soften a little as she heard the concern in Gemma's voice and the sharpness in her tone disappeared.

"Ahhh I see. Well I think Katee should come to the sick bay until I can phone her parents. If one of you could come with me, you can give me some more information about her so that we can get her home as quickly as possible."

While the nurse bent down to help Katee, Melissa turned to Gemma.

"You go with Katee and I'll explain to everyone where you are. I just hope she's going to be alright you know? Meet me when you know any more yeah?"

"Okay Mel," Gemma replied. "If I don't see you before, I'll definitely meet you at lunch time. Erm…let's meet in the classroom okay?"

"Could one of you girls give me a hand here so that we can get Katee up?"

Gemma responded immediately to the nurse as Melissa disappeared into the classroom. With one person on either side of her, Katee walked very shakily down the corridor to the sick bay. Her mind felt muddy and slow as she tried to remember exactly what had happened.

She remembered leaving Gemma when Melissa appeared. She'd suddenly felt threatened and needed to escape. Hiding in a toilet cubicle, she felt engulfed by loneliness. Why had she just done that? Why had she scurried away as soon as another person appeared? As if from nowhere, the 'voice' in her head started to answer her questions.

"I'll tell you why you ran away. It's because you KNOW that if you get friendly with these people, they'll discover your secret. They'll make you eat. They won't leave you alone to diet and will feed you enormous meals. They'll buy you chocolate and force you to eat crisps. You'll just get fatter and fatter and fatter and fatter until you're HUGE!"

"STOP!!!" Katee yelled out loud.

The shock of hearing her own voice in the silent toilets had jolted her back to reality. Katee had started to hate this internal 'voice' that taunted her about food all the time. It told her how to behave and issued her with strict instructions. It told her not to eat and that she mustn't speak to other people. It said that she had to exercise and starve herself until she was thinner. At first it had helped to have the 'voice' to keep her under control. When the hunger was unbearable, it kept her fighting on. It had felt like a friend. Her only friend. But slowly, it was becoming the enemy. However much she wanted to eat, she knew that the 'voice' simply wouldn't let her. It sounded crazy to say that she was controlled by an inner 'voice' but she knew that she was. How could she ever explain that to anyone though? This was a secret she had to keep… forever.

The silence in the toilets reminded Katee that she was late for registration and she hurriedly left the basement and started to run up the stairs. She still felt tired from all the exercise of the previous night but the 'voice' wouldn't let her rest. She heard it's taunts to run faster and she pushed herself to race up the steep steps to her second floor classroom.

She could remember the stairs and the 'voice'. She could remember seeing her classroom door at the end of the corridor. She could remember feeling sick and a little dizzy but that was where her memories ended. What had happened? She had to know.

By the time the three of them reached the sick bay, Katee was feeling a little steadier on her feet and only wanted to be left alone. She couldn't have any fuss. She had to get back to class and carry on as normal.

"I'm sorry for causing so much trouble but…I'm fine now thanks," she said to the nurse. "I just tripped up I think…I've got to get back to my class before I miss any more of my lesson."

However the nurse disagreed.

"Oh no young lady. You're not going anywhere for a while. You just fainted and that's quite serious. You need to go home for a rest and then make an appointment with your doctor for a check up."

Katee started to panic. She couldn't see a doctor because he might weigh her and her mother mustn't know she had fainted because she might make her eat more. She had to think fast.

"I'm fine…honestly nurse. I've…got my period at the moment, which often makes me feel dizzy and faint. I do bleed quite heavily and I guess it was just…just a bit too much for me."

Katee knew this was a blatant lie. She hadn't had her period for over ten weeks now. She had tried to pretend to herself that she was still fine but she was beginning to feel frightened. She didn't know what was happening to her body and wanted to talk to someone but the 'voice' wouldn't let her. She had to keep everything a secret and the school nurse just couldn't be allowed to spoil everything.

"You need to see a doctor Katee and I'm going to phone your mother immediately to tell her what's happened," the nurse continued. "Did you have any breakfast this morning?"

The dreaded subject of food had finally been mentioned and Katee felt fear and anger flood through her whole body. Her face reddened and the voice she spoke with was fierce and determined.

"Look, why don't you just leave me alone? I ate breakfast, okay? And I don't appreciate you interfering in my life. I'm feeling better and I want to go back to my classroom."

These words filled Gemma with a sense of dread. This was the Katee she'd seen in the classroom. The angry young girl who hated anyone that questioned her about food or eating. Another piece of the jigsaw slotted into place in Gemma's mind but she still needed time to think. She wanted to help Katee but just blurting out random thoughts wouldn't help anyone. She had to think and she also needed to talk to Melissa.

The nurse had ignored Katee's outburst and could now be heard talking quietly on a distant phone. Gemma looked over at Katee and felt helpless. She wanted to say something to make her feel better but she didn't know what. She felt inadequate and tried to wrack her brains for the right words.

Finally, Katee spoke and Gemma could hear the desperation in her voice.

"Gemma…help me. Please. I can't see a doctor. I just can't. What…what should I do?"

Gemma's heart went out to her.

"Oh Katee…it'll be okay. Doctors aren't that bad you know. If you have a good one, they can really help. If it's just period problems then they'll be able to give you some pills or something to make it better."

The plea for help changed back to an angry dismissal when Katee realised that Gemma didn't have a solution. Turning her head away, she snapped back sarcastically.

"Great! That's so much help Gemma. If you can't say anything useful then why don't you just go away and leave me alone?"

As soon as she had spoken, Katee was riddled with guilt. Why did she snap so much these days? She'd always been so mild-tempered in the past but now she was filled with rage at a moment's notice. She hated the person she was becoming and felt ashamed of her ungrateful behaviour. She was convinced that Gemma would hate her now and she couldn't even bring herself to look up. The quiet, gentle voice she heard in response to her outburst shocked her.

"I'm sorry I can't help you Katee. I want to help – you can always talk to me."

The kindness was almost too much for Katee to bear and hot tears started to drip onto her lap. It seemed such a long time since anyone had really cared. She felt a piece of paper thrust into her hand as Gemma's quiet words continued.

"This is my phone number. You can ring me any time."

As she left the sick bay, Gemma's mind was filled with questions and thoughts. She wanted to go to the library that night and find a book on eating disorders. If her fears were correct then she would be better prepared if she knew some more facts. She hoped that Katee would be okay but had no idea whether she had understanding parents or a good doctor. Was her home life good or bad? Was there anyone she could turn to?

Gemma walked down the empty corridor to her classroom. Out of the corner of her eye, she noticed that a small book was sticking out from under a display table. She reached down to rescue the book, knowing just how annoying it was to lose a textbook. As she picked it up, she realised it wasn't a textbook but was actually a small notebook or even a diary. She opened the first page to see who had lost such an important possession and the words 'KATEE QUINN'S JOURNAL – PRIVATE' leapt out at her.

The book must have fallen out of Katee's bag when she fainted. Gemma knew she would be frantic when she realised it was lost but how could she return it without arousing any suspicion? If a teacher or nurse saw the book, they might flick through it and read Katee's private thoughts. Gemma shoved the book into her bag and walked into the classroom. Now she really needed to talk to Melissa.

12
The Phone Call Home

When Jane Quinn received the phone call from her daughter's school, she left work immediately. Although she hated taking time off because her boss was quite difficult, she had no choice. Brian was on a training day for his new job and that meant she was the only one available to pick up their daughter. She was very concerned about Katee. She couldn't exactly put her finger on it but she knew that something just wasn't right. Katee had certainly lost a lot of weight since the summer holidays.

The nurse had said that Katee had fainted and she'd advised Jane to take her to their family doctor. Jane's mind drifted back over the last few months. She knew that Brian hadn't been treating Katee particularly well for a while. Since he'd lost his job, he hadn't really behaved very well towards anyone but it was definitely their daughter who had been treated the worst. Perhaps she should talk with him about being a bit gentler. Katee was a very intelligent girl and she knew that Brian expected great things from her but he really didn't need to push her so hard. The trouble was that he'd set his sights on a top University for her and was certain that she could achieve this goal. This was why his temper flared every time her marks were a little lower than he expected. However, she knew she had to explain to him that all that really mattered was their daughter's health and happiness. After all, she might not even want to go to University. Brian hadn't even stopped to ask Katee what she had in mind for the future.

As Jane arrived at the school, she also promised herself that she would find more time to talk with Katee. She realised that she barely saw her child any more. Katee always seemed to be tucked away in her bedroom studying and that needed to change. In the past, they'd always had a good mother/daughter relationship but it looked like that needed some work now. Jane decided she would make a real effort to get to know her daughter again.

She arrived at the sick bay, knocked on the door and heard a voice call out. Opening the door, she was greeted by the nurse.

"Hello Mrs. Quinn. Can I have a quick word before you take Katee home?"

Jane nodded in agreement and the nurse ushered her into a small office.

"Do have a seat," the nurse said in a friendly voice, pointing towards a comfortable lounge chair. "I asked you in here because I'm a little concerned about Katee. I've taken her pulse and it's much slower than normal. Her temperature is also lower than average and she's very pale. Have you noticed any changes in your daughter recently Mrs. Quinn?"

"Well she has lost a bit of weight in the last few months but I just put that down to a growth spurt. You know how teenagers suddenly reach that long and leggy stage?" Jane smiled and paused momentarily. "Thinking about it though, she has been a lot quieter lately and she is very conscientious. I wonder if the pressure of the GCSE year is a bit much for her? Sixteen isn't an easy age is it?"

"Katee certainly could be struggling with the pressure," the nurse agreed. "Many teenagers do feel a strong need to achieve good results. They're always being told that jobs are scarce and that good qualifications are essential. Part of my job is to watch the girls to see that they're not getting too stressed. Drug taking, smoking and eating disorders are all possible 'escape routes' for teenagers under pressure."

The nurse spoke knowledgeably and Jane shuddered. It couldn't be that serious with Katee. Surely it was just a little stress. The nurse had to be overreacting. It was her next question that really startled Jane though. "Mrs. Quinn, I'm wondering if Katee may have a problem with food? I mentioned breakfast to her and she became very defensive. I think it may be wise for you to have a gentle word with her."

For a second, Jane had trouble catching her breath. She hadn't even wanted to face the possibility that Katee might have a serious problem with food and eating. She'd tried to block out her fears by telling herself that all teenage girls became picky over food. However, when she thought back over the last few months, she couldn't really remember seeing Katee eat much at all. Up until just before the summer holidays, Katee had loved crisps and was always asking if she could have another packet. Recently though, she'd noticed that the crisps just sat in the cupboard until David or Brian ate them. She also remembered that she never bought Katee special treats any more. She'd tried to buy tubs of ice cream or chocolate bars but always found that they were left unopened and so in time, she just gave up even buying them. Could her daughter really have an eating disorder of some kind?

Jane turned to the nurse and thanked her for her help.

"Is it alright if I take my daughter home now? Do I need to sign anything?"

"No Mrs. Quinn. That's fine. Do please let us know if Katee needs time off school though and remember, if I can help, just phone me."

The nurse then took Jane through to the small clinic area where Katee was resting. As she looked at her daughter, Jane tried not to cry out. Her daughter looked so young and defenceless, curled up into a tight ball on the fold out bed. Her colour was very pale and she looked so tiny.

"Katee? Wake up love. I'm going to take you home."

Katee opened her eyes and looked sadly at her mother. She wanted to reach out for a comforting hug but she felt torn. Part of her wanted help because she was scared and alone but the other part wanted to push everyone away.

As she walked with her Mum to the car, Katee suddenly felt nervous. She knew how important her Mum's job was and she hated the fact that she'd made her take time off. Would Dad be angry? Would her parents argue? All she seemed to do recently was cause tension at home. Looking sideways, Katee studied her Mum. She didn't seem angry – just very concerned.

When they were both seated in the car, Jane finally turned to her daughter.

"Well love, I really think we need to talk. Is there anything you want to tell me?"

"No Mum, I don't think so. I just felt a bit faint today. I'm fine. Really I am."

"I don't think you are Katee and neither did the nurse. I'm going to make you an appointment with Dr. Morgan for this evening. I think you should have a check up."

"No Mum! No! You CAN'T do that!"

Jane was shocked by the ferocity of her daughter's anger. Her eyes were blazing with fury and there were two bright spots of colour in her cheeks. The nurse had warned her that Katee might be very defensive if a doctor's appointment was mentioned but she hadn't expected this much hostility.

"I'm sorry Katee but I have to take you to the doctors today. It's just not negotiable. You need a check up and we also need to talk about how much you're eating."

"I'm eating fine Mum. All I want is for people to leave me alone. This year's important for me and I can't afford to miss any school. I don't need a doctor! I don't need to take time off today and I don't need to eat more food!"

Katee started to scrabble for the door. She had to escape from everyone. Running away was the only option left. She had no idea where she would run to but she knew that she needed to be alone. Alone with just the 'voice'.

Jane grabbed her daughter as she tried to leave and pulled her back into the car. Gently turning her around, Jane hugged her child to her. She felt a shiver of fear run down her spine as she realised just how much weight Katee had lost. Through the many layers of clothing that Katee was wearing, Jane could feel sharp bones protruding. As she hugged her daughter to her, she talked quietly in a reassuring voice. She sounded confident and strong, telling Katee that they would cope with any problems she had. Inside she didn't feel so sure though. She'd heard that teenage girls died from eating disorders and Katee seemed so fiercely determined to fight everyone who tried to help. Would she be able to help her daughter if there really was a problem?

Pushing her fears to one side, Jane realised she was jumping ahead of herself. Katee had only been losing weight for a few months. Surely her problem couldn't be that serious yet. They needed to take it all one step at a time. She gave Katee a final squeeze and started the car.

"Come on honey. We need to get you home for a rest and then I'm making that appointment. I'll come with you okay? I promise you won't have to face this alone."

Katee sat in her seat and fumed. Staring blankly out of the window, she raged silently against her mother. Why wouldn't everyone just give her a break? She wasn't the least bit thin. In fact, she was still massively fat. She needed to lose a lot more weight. Visiting the doctor would be a total waste of time because he would just confirm that she was fat. At that moment she hated everyone and the 'voice' seemed like the only one that understood her.

"If you see the doctor, he'll make you eat more. Everyone's going to make you eat more. They hate you and want to make your life a misery. People are becoming suspicious and they'll start to watch you. Your life won't be your own any more and you'll grow larger and larger until you're just a HUGE FAT BLOB!"

The words were shouted so loudly that Katee almost wanted to cover her ears. But then the voice spoke more quietly.

"I can help you though. I can give you some good ideas that will save you from all that weight gain. If you listen to me, everything will be fine."

The 'voice' had the answer to all her problems. A sense of relief flooded through Katee. It was going to be alright. If she just listened to the 'voice' then everything would be fine…

13
Disclosure

Gemma had to wait until lunch time before she could finally talk with Melissa alone. As soon as she saw her friend, Gemma started talking at a hundred miles an hour. All her ideas and thoughts poured out in a jumble and Melissa struggled to understand.

"Gemma! Gemma! You're gonna have to slow down. I can't follow what you're saying. You think Katee's got anorexia? But that's such a serious illness. Sure, Katee's lost a bit of weight but she isn't crazy or anything."

"Mel, people with anorexia aren't crazy. They're just ill," Gemma said seriously. "Yeah, it's a very serious illness but it's not that rare you know? There was an anorexic girl at my last school and I learnt a bit about the illness then. I really want to get a book out of the library so that I can learn more but I do remember that it's all about being insecure. I think that anorexics don't feel they deserve to eat food because they believe that they're bad people. Well that's how it was for this girl I knew…Carrie Lewis. She hated herself and just wanted to disappear. Even though she was really thin, she actually thought she was fat."

"Do you think Katee believes she's fat?" Melissa asked in amazement. "But that's crazy. Now I'm fat and I know it but Katee? Are you sure Gemma?"

"Well I haven't been able to ask her that yet but every time anyone tries to talk to her about food or eating, she just shouts at them. Remember how she yelled at me when I asked her to go to lunch? Well she did that again and worse when we were in the sick bay. I don't think she's doing it deliberately though. I just think she's really terrified of eating."

"Whoa! That's amazing Gemma. Why would anyone be afraid of food? I've got exactly the opposite problem. I just can't seem to cut down. I do try but I just end up pigging out."

Horrified, Melissa realised that she had just let out one of her deepest secrets – the fact that she privately binged. She started to apologise frantically for her behaviour.

"Oh no! You're going to think I'm disgusting now aren't you Gemma? I mean, look at you. You obviously don't have a problem with food and you're such a lovely size and shape. But me? Well I'm just disgusting aren't I? I'm hippo size. A balloon on legs. I try to diet but I always seem to get so hungry. I can't even imagine how Katee starves herself."

Gemma smiled at Melissa and then walked over to give her a hug.

"Of course I don't think you're disgusting. I understand. I really do." More than you know, Gemma thought to herself. "Everyone on a diet gets hungry and pigs out sometimes. Thanks for telling me though Mel. Hey, maybe I can help you with your diet. I'm on kind of a diet myself at the moment."

"You're on a diet Gemma? But why? You don't need to lose weight any more than Katee does. I just don't understand what's happening to everyone."

Gemma wished that she could tell Melissa the whole truth about the 'diet' she was on. She hated the bingeing and vomiting but how could she ever tell anyone about it? She had to sort it out herself. She would just decide never to do it again and that would be that. If she concentrated on helping her two new friends, she could block out her own silly problems.

"I really need to go to the library Mel but not the school one," Gemma announced after a moment's silence. "Would you like to come with me?"

"I want to Gemma but I can't," Melissa said, sounding disappointed. "I need to visit my Dad in hospital after school."

Gemma felt annoyed with herself for forgetting about Melissa's father. Katee's problem had just pushed it from her mind.

"Oh Mel I'm so sorry. I forgot all about that. How about if we go down to the corner shop and buy him a card?"

Melissa smiled. She was dreading the hospital visit that evening and she'd been trying to work out when she could buy her Dad a small gift.

"That'd be great Gemma. We could pick up some fruit too while we're there."

∞∞∞∞

The afternoon passed slowly for the two girls and they both found it impossible to concentrate on their classes. Gemma kept remembering bits and pieces of information about anorexia. She'd been strongly affected by the incident at her previous school when the girl in the year above her had fallen ill with the disorder. No one had noticed for months that Carrie Lewis was slowly losing weight and by the time they did discover her secret, she was dangerously ill. She had been admitted to a general hospital and tube fed for many weeks. Her weight had risen but as soon as she was released from the hospital, she lost all the weight she'd gained.

Gemma remembered hearing that Carrie was waiting for a bed in an eating disorders unit so that she could receive the specialist help she needed. Then one morning, an announcement was made in assembly.

At the age of just 16, Carrie had died of a heart attack. Gemma had not been able to believe what she'd heard and had started to ask questions. The school buzzed with the news for days and the headteacher arranged for a nurse to come and talk with the students about the dangers of eating disorders. Gemma hadn't realised that anorexia was so dangerous until Carrie had died and she'd tried to find out as much information as possible. As time passed though, the memory of Carrie's death had faded a little. Other problems had started to fill Gemma's head and then there'd been the news that they were moving house.

Gemma's mother had only been a deputy headteacher at her former school and when she was offered the promotion at Weatherbrook High, the decision was an easy one for her. The new job came with a healthy pay rise and Clare Williams was certain the move would be beneficial for both herself and her daughter. Gemma wasn't so sure though. She hated the idea of leaving her friends behind and joining a new school when everyone else was already in groups. As soon as she'd heard about the move and the change of school, she started dieting even more fiercely. She was terrified of being teased or bullied because she wasn't as thin as the other girls. She knew that Weatherbrook High was a more exclusive school in a smarter area of town. She didn't want to be seen as frumpy and dowdy in comparison with the other girls. Now she had two reasons to lose weight. It wasn't just to make her Mum proud any more.

Gemma knew that her mother was excited about the move to a better school. She wanted her daughter to have the best education possible and that meant she often pressured Gemma about her marks. Gemma did work hard but however much extra time she put in, the best she received were 'B' grades. She just wasn't a straight 'A' student and that constantly upset her Mum. This left Gemma feeling a failure and instead of being pleased with her 'B' grades, she always felt inadequate.

"Are you with us Gemma Williams? GEMMA WILLIAMS!"

Gemma realised too late that the teacher must have been talking to her for a number of minutes. She looked at the blackboard and couldn't understand any of the mathematical symbols that were written down. Before she could stop herself, words started tumbling out of her mouth.

"I'm sorry Miss. I really wasn't paying attention."

Miss Evans stared at her student in amazement.

"So my lesson is too boring for you is it Gemma? Well perhaps you'll find it a little more interesting after you've spent some time in detention this afternoon."

"But Miss…I can't have detention tonight."

"Yes you can Gemma and you will. I'll go and see your mother immediately after this lesson. Isn't it handy that she's the headmistress and I don't have to give you the usual 24 hours notice? Maybe in future it will remind you to pay a little more attention in my classes."

Gemma sunk down lower in her seat. Detention always lasted an hour, which would leave her only forty minutes to reach the library before it closed. Why did nothing seem to go right for her at the moment? She looked up to see Melissa giving her a sympathetic smile. Well it wasn't all bad. At least she seemed to have found a friend in Mel and she smiled back warmly.

14
The First Appointment

Katee looked around the waiting room. She still could not believe she was about to see a doctor. The arguments that afternoon had been intense but her mother had held a firm line. She wanted Katee to see the doctor and no amount of anger or tears would change that. Katee was terrified. Her stomach was churning and her heart was racing. She had bundled herself up in many layers of clothing to try and hide her weight loss but she still felt vulnerable. A hundred different thoughts ran through her mind. What questions would the doctor ask? Would he run any tests? Would he notice her weight loss?

And then she heard a voice.

"Katee Quinn to see Dr. Morgan please."

Katee couldn't move. She tried to get up but her legs just wouldn't work. She could see her mother standing in front of her but felt she was in a dream.

"Katee, come on. It's your turn to see the doctor," Jane said, slightly impatiently. "Do you need a hand?"

She felt her mother pulling her arm, trying to help her up. A nurse appeared beside her and took her other arm. Katee's legs were shaking. They didn't feel as though they even belonged to her. With help, she was taken into the doctor's surgery where she was settled into a seat opposite the doctor. She then listened while her mother described what had happened that day. Katee felt annoyed. Why did everyone keep saying she was thin and not eating? She was just on a diet because she was too fat. Couldn't they understand that?

When her mother stopped speaking, the doctor turned to Katee.

"I think I should start by weighing you Katee. Will you slip off your coat, jumper and shoes please?"

Katee recoiled in horror. She had planned on being weighed in all her clothes. She couldn't take anything off. Frozen to the spot, she just stared at the doctor.

"Do you need any help with your clothes Katee? I can call in the nurse if you want."

The idea of being undressed like a small child felt even more demeaning and Katee slowly started to remove her shoes. At the same time, she tried to reason with the doctor.

"I really don't need to be weighed. I'm absolutely fine. I haven't lost any weight."

"It's good that you haven't lost any weight Katee but I still need to weigh you." Dr. Morgan smiled reassuringly. "Do you know the last measurements I have for you are from when you were only nine and that was over six years ago? I think I need to update my notes a bit don't you?"

Katee realised she'd been backed into a corner. She could argue all day and still the doctor would insist that she was weighed. She looked angrily at the set of scales in the corner of the room. She hated them. She wished she could just pick them up and throw them out of the window but something stopped her. There was still a part of her that wanted to please everyone all the time and which stopped her from behaving that badly.

"Okay Katee, are you ready?" the doctor asked. "Oh that shirt looks heavy too. Can you slip it off as well please?"

Katee felt almost naked as she walked towards the scales. She clutched her arms tightly around her upper body in an attempt to hide herself from the gaze of her mother and the doctor. She stood in front of the scales and stared at the weighing apparatus.

"Katee, I realise that you don't want to stand on the scales but I need to know your weight," the doctor explained. "I can't let you go home until I know what it is. Come on. It'll be over before you know it."

Katee knew she was beaten. She had no choice. She stepped slowly onto the scales and watched the needle gradually rise.

"Okay. Let me see what we have here," Dr. Morgan said as he bent forward so that he could accurately read the result.

Katee wanted to push his head out of the way because it was blocking her view of the reading. What did the scales say? She had to know.

"Right Katee, step off the scales please."

Katee remained standing on the scales, motionless like a stone statue. She couldn't move until she had seen the reading. These scales were different to the set at home and the measurement was in kilogrammes, which she didn't understand. She was used to stones and pounds.

"Katee, please put on your clothes and come over here and sit down again. I need to talk with you and your mother," Dr. Morgan said with authority.

Katee pulled on her clothes and shoes. The number she'd seen on the scales was burned into her memory. What did it mean? She wished she knew how many pounds there were in a kilogramme. She had to remember that figure so that she could look it up as soon as she got home.

When she was finally seated, the doctor started talking and fear began to surge through Katee's body again.

"Right. Well I think we have a bit of a problem here," the doctor said. His expression was solemn as he directed his comments to Jane. "Katee's weight is not good. She's very underweight for her age and height and I think there may be something seriously wrong."

He turned to Katee and continued talking.

"I want to do some more tests to see if there's a physical problem that I'm missing. I also want to see if your dieting has caused any damage to your body. Our bodies need food Katee and if you don't give it the right amount then it literally starts to eat itself. It feeds off muscle and because your heart is the biggest muscle in your body, in time it will eat away at this too. I need you to have some tests done to see if your heart is damaged in any way. I'll give you a card to take to the hospital where they'll give you an ECG. That stands for electrocardiogram. But don't worry. It's not painful."

Katee couldn't believe what was happening to her. She had been so certain that the doctor would say there wasn't a problem. She knew that she was fat so why was everyone saying that she was thin? Then she heard the words she had dreaded more than anything.

"I want your mother to monitor your diet from now on Katee. We need to make sure that you're eating enough calories each day. A young woman of your age who's still growing needs at least 2,000 calories a day. I have a selection of diet sheets here that I'll give to both you and your

Mum. They explain about good nutrition and show you the different food types. For example here look," he said, pointing to one of the sheets. "It says that you need to eat nine servings of carbohydrates each day."

"NINE?" Katee repeated the word in disbelief. "You've got to be kidding!"

"That's really not so much Katee," the doctor calmly continued. "For instance, one serving of carbohydrates is just a slice of bread. So if you have one round of sandwiches with margarine and cheese, you've already eaten two servings of carbohydrates, one serving of fat and one serving of protein. Do you see how it works? It's almost a game to make sure you have the correct amount of nutrition each day."

Katee certainly didn't think this was a game of any kind. In fact it felt like she was living through a nightmare. She could hear the 'voice' inside her yelling loudly. It was screaming at her, drowning out everyone else in the room. She realised her mother and the doctor were still speaking but she couldn't hear a word they were saying. The 'voice' had taken control.

"You can't do what they say! If you eat TWO THOUSAND CALORIES a day you'll become MASSIVE! You still have SO much weight to lose. You mustn't listen to that doctor. He doesn't know what he's talking about. They all hate you and just want to make you FAT! If you listen to me, I'll help you to lose more weight. I'll show you how to beat everyone and become thin. I know that's what you really want."

"Katee? Katee? Did you hear what the doctor said?"

Mrs. Quinn was gently shaking her daughter's shoulder. The 'voice' in Katee's head faded again and she turned angry eyes onto her mother.

"What?" she snapped fiercely.

"Katee! Don't take that tone love. The doctor was saying that he wants to see you once a week for a while. He needs to monitor your weight to make sure you start gaining."

Katee didn't answer her mother but just stared at the floor. The 'voice' had said it would help her to lose more weight and show her ways to become thin. The 'voice' would help her to beat the doctor. Why did everyone have to push her all the time to become something she didn't want to be? All she wanted was to be thin. What was so bad about that? There were plenty of girls at school who were much thinner than she was and their mothers didn't drag them to the doctors. It was all so unfair.

She realised that the doctor was talking to her again.

"Okay Katee. This is the card you need to take with you to the hospital tomorrow morning. It requests a number of blood tests and an ECG to check your heart rate. When you come and see me next week I should have the results back and then I'll know more."

Katee could hear her Mum thanking the doctor and reassuring him that she would take her daughter along to the hospital in the morning. At that moment, she didn't want to talk to anyone and stormed out of the surgery without saying another word. She was furious again. She hated feeling this way but she just couldn't help it. Her mother talked quietly to her as they drove home but Katee refused to answer. At that moment she hated her mother.

When they arrived home, Mrs. Quinn switched off the car engine and turned to look at her daughter's angry face. She wanted to comfort Katee but knew that they both needed time to adjust. There was a light on in the house and Jane realised that Brian was home. Telling her husband about their daughter's serious weight loss was not going to be easy. Would he understand that Katee was not trying to be difficult but actually had an illness? They would both need to show her kindness and support but Jane wasn't sure that he would understand that. He expected so much of his little girl. She stopped her daughter before she got out of the car.

"Katee I need to explain a few things to your father. Why don't you go upstairs for a while? I'll come and get you when dinner's ready."

"I don't WANT any dinner!" Katee shouted.

She felt like a spoilt child, stamping her foot and screaming but she was unable to stop herself.

"Katee, I know you don't want to eat," Jane said calmly. "But you need to have something. I promise I'll make you a light meal. I know this is hard for you so we'll take it really easy. Now go and have a rest until I call you, okay?"

Katee slammed out of the car without another word to her mother. She headed straight for her room, ignoring the shouted hellos from her brother and father. The 'voice' had started speaking again and although its words were frightening, she knew that she had to follow its instructions if she was to feel better.

"You feel bad don't you Katee? You hate feeling so angry and being so difficult towards your Mum? Do you feel like a bad person? Do you feel you need to punish yourself? I know something that will make you feel better. It will take away the pain you feel inside."

Katee couldn't quite believe what the 'voice' was saying but it did seem to make sense. Yes, she did feel a need to punish herself for being angry and difficult. She was also in so much pain that she just wanted it to go away. Following the voice's instructions, she walked over to her sewing box and found her sharpest needle. Very carefully she rolled up her left sleeve and looked down at her arm. It was so fat and ugly. She hated it so much. She felt nervous and wanted to stop but the 'voice' in her head continued to talk, quietly encouraging her.

"Go on Katee. Don't stop now. Do it. It'll make you feel better. I promise that it'll take away the pain."

Katee looked again at the needle and then at her arm. Her hand was shaking but she had to trust the 'voice'. It wanted to help her didn't it? She gritted her teeth, closed her eyes and braced herself for the pain.

15
The Library

Gemma arrived at the library, hot and out of breath. Looking at her watch, she saw with relief that she still had half an hour before it closed. She pushed her way through the main doors and stood still for a minute while her eyes adjusted to the dark, musty atmosphere. She loved libraries. Books had always been an escape for her. She would disappear into different worlds and forget her own worries as she lived each story with its characters.

She decided to start looking for books on eating disorders in the health section. When she found the section covering food-related problems though, she felt disappointed. Although there were four wide shelves filled with books about how to diet, there were only three books specifically about eating disorders. Grabbing the textbooks, she moved over to the reading section and found a chair in a quiet corner. She opened the first one and started to read. Sentences began to leap out at her from the pages.

"Anorexia is a very secretive illness and anorexics often feel ashamed of their behaviour and try to pretend that there is nothing wrong. However, it is obvious when someone is suffering from this disorder because it involves severe weight loss...

People with anorexia seem to lose confidence and start to become quieter and more withdrawn than usual, often isolating themselves from their friends and family...

The sufferer has a terrible fear of becoming fat and cannot see how thin they really are. They often start to wear many layers of baggy clothing, not only because they want to hide their body but also because they are very cold...

Over time, the sufferer grows more frail and their skin becomes pale, with deep black shadows appearing under their eyes. Fainting and dizziness are common problems and anaemia is another side effect of anorexia...

Sufferers often feel moody and irritable and may become snappy with friends and family...

They often appear to be high achievers and always try to get good grades at school."

The more Gemma read, the dryer her mouth became. This book could have been written about Katee. She had all the symptoms. Any lingering doubts about her friend's illness had just disappeared.

"Are you alright? Can I help at all? The library's closing and I'm afraid I will have to ask you to leave."

Gemma looked up into two deep hazel eyes.

"Oh I'm so sorry...erm... " Looking at his badge, Gemma read the name 'Tim Rosen – Assistant Librarian'. "Um...Tim, I think I just lost track of the time."

"That's not a problem. I just wondered if you were okay. You look a bit shocked."

"Yeah, I just discovered something about a friend and it's kinda freaked me. I mean I suspected but actually knowing is...different, you know? But you really don't want to know all this do you? Sorry, I'm keeping you from going home."

"That's okay. I'm in no rush and I am interested. Look, why don't I check these out?" Tim said, pointing to her books. "Then if you like, we could get a coffee in the shop over the road and you could tell me about your friend...if you want to that is."

"Erm...well I...er...I...er...I don't know." Gemma was annoyed that she sounded so uncertain but this kind of thing didn't happen to her. Men in libraries didn't just ask her out.

"Oh that's okay. It was only a suggestion. I can understand that you're a bit nervous about going for coffee with a complete stranger. Look, I'll just check your books and let you go home."

"No!" Gemma suddenly said in a voice that was slightly too loud. What harm could she come to in a busy coffee shop with a librarian? "I'd like to go for a coffee. It'd be good to talk to someone about all this."

Five minutes later, Gemma was sitting in a comfy chair, sipping a steaming cappuccino and explaining the whole story to Tim.

"… and when she fainted, the pieces started to fall into place. I remembered Carrie from my last school and it's horrible to see how similar Katee looks. All of this just made me sure I had to find out more. You talked to me just after I'd found this book and read some of the symptoms of anorexia. They describe Katee so perfectly. Look. Let me show you."

Gemma reached down into her bag and started shuffling through her schoolbooks so that she could find the textbook she'd just been reading. Her hand touched a book she didn't recognise and she gasped when she realised it was Katee's diary.

Tim heard her sharp intake of breath.

"What's wrong Gemma?"

"It's Katee's diary. I rescued it from the corridor outside our classroom this morning. It must have fallen out of Katee's bag when she fainted. I know it would answer so many questions but I can't look in it. That just wouldn't be right. I mean it's a privacy thing isn't it? You can't go looking in people's diaries. I'd kill anyone who looked in mine. It'd just be so embarrassing. But at the same time, I know I could help Katee if I knew more about what she was thinking…"

Tim looked thoughtful while he stirred his coffee.

"I don't really know anything about eating disorders but I do know that trust is a really important part of friendship. If Katee suspected that you'd read her diary, I think she'd probably run a mile. I mean you were saying that anorexics are very secretive anyway and this book's full of

Katee's private thoughts and feelings. You need to wait until she shows it to you before you can discuss it with her."

"I know you're right Tim. I guess I just don't really know how to return the book to her without embarrassing her though. I mean she doesn't really know me yet so maybe she'll assume I've looked inside anyway. I had to open the first page to see whose book it was. What if she thinks I read the whole thing?"

"Well I guess you'll just have to explain that to her. It sounds like she needs a friend right now and you're the one person she did try to reach out to. I know as soon as you offered her advice, she turned it down but she tried to talk and that's a good sign isn't it?"

"Yeah, I think so. It did say in this book that the first stage of recovery is recognising that you've got a problem and then asking for help. I don't think Katee's quite there yet but maybe a little part of her wants help. I wonder how she got on at the doctors today."

Tim's face lit up as a new thought occurred to him.

"Hey I've got an idea. Why don't you ask her about that appointment and then say that you found her diary? I think it's just gonna have to be a trust thing. Say that you found it and then made sure that no one looked in it. Tell her what you told me about how important privacy is and how you'd kill anyone that read your diary."

"Hmmm. You're right Tim. It's the best I can do anyway. Thanks. You've been a real help. I guess I still don't really have a clue about how to help Katee but I want to read these books and see if they give me any ideas."

"Why do you think it started Gemma?"

Gemma looked confused by the question.

"Sorry Tim? Why did what start?"

"Katee's anorexia. I mean you don't just wake up with it one morning do you? Even I know that much."

"Yeah. Good question Tim. Hang on. Let me have a flick through this book again."

When she found the chapter that covered why eating disorders started, Katee began to read.

"Okay listen to this…

For most people the eating disorder is a way of blocking out their problems…

Eating disorders are illnesses about control. When a person feels out of control in their life and unable to solve a problem, an eating disorder can seem like the answer. This is often the case for people who are being abused.

Whoa Tim. Do you think Katee could have been abused?"

"Hang on a minute there Gemma," Tim said seriously. "You can't go jumping to any conclusions. You're just skimming that book at the moment and there's bound to be loads of other reasons why it starts. You can't assume that Katee's been abused just because she's got anorexia. Doesn't it give you any other reasons there?"

"Hold on, let me look. Erm… YEAH. Here's another reason…

Some young girls turn to anorexia because they feel too afraid of growing up. Adulthood brings many new and quite frightening changes… and they feel too afraid of the responsibility of being an adult.

Hmmm," Gemma pondered. "That's interesting but Katee seems quite adult already, if you know what I mean. There are some really baby kids in my new class but Katee's kind of…mature and older than her years. Does that make any sense?"

Tim nodded and Gemma carried on reading.

"Hey this bit's interesting…

If children are not allowed to express their opinions but are simply expected to take on their parents ideas, they do not find their own identity… they may use an eating disorder as their identity instead.

You know Tim, I think I'm gonna have to get to know Katee's parents and her family situation a bit better. In fact, I think I really need to know her a lot better altogether. Wow! There's so many reasons here why eating disorders develop. Look – the death of a family member, parents divorcing, a need for attention, a trauma such as a car accident, loneliness… It could be any of them. I only hope I can get Katee to trust me before she gets any worse. It says here that the earlier you catch an eating disorder, the easier it is to beat. Maybe I'm just being crazy but I really want to help Katee beat this."

Tim looked at the intense girl opposite him. It was amazing. She seemed to have such a determined and caring nature. If anyone was likely to be able to help this Katee then he thought it would probably be Gemma. He smiled at her. She was a rare kind of person. One who worried about others and tried to help. So many of the people he knew just seemed to ignore everyone else's problems and live their own busy lives.

As he watched Gemma flick through the book, his mind started to wander. He had wanted to talk to her for at least a month now. She visited the library at least twice a week and recently he'd found himself watching for her to arrive. He'd only been working at the library a few months himself and Gemma had joined soon after he began work. It was just a temporary job because he was taking a year off before he went to University. He really wanted to travel but needed to save up some money before he could just take off anywhere. For a temporary job though it was fun. He'd always loved books and was quite happy working amongst them all day.

Tim suddenly realised that Gemma had put away the book and was staring at him curiously.

"You okay Tim? You disappeared on me. And why do you have that goofy grin on your face?"

"Goofy grin? I don't have a goofy grin. I'm…cool and sophisticated," he replied, trying to look aloof.

Gemma couldn't stifle the loud laugh that immediately escaped when she heard his words. Cute and understanding maybe but sophisticated?

"Erm…not in those jeans and shirt Tim. You can't be sophisticated in an old man's shirt."

"It is not an old man's shirt Gemma. It's regulation library wear and I'll have you know that cool and sophisticated isn't just about clothes. It's all about your attitude."

"Whoa. Aren't we the learned one Mr. Timothy Rosen? Sounds like you've read every book in the library."

They giggled together and Gemma couldn't quite believe what was happening. Any shyness she'd originally felt had just disappeared and she was happy and comfortable there with Tim. Looking at the clock in the corner of the shop, she was amazed to see they'd been talking for over an hour. She felt disappointed but knew she had to leave or else her Mum would worry.

"Tim, I'm sorry but I really have to go. It's been…er…really great. Thanks for the coffee. Oh and of course for the help with Katee. Do you… er…maybe want me to let you know what happens with her?" she finished shyly.

"Oh yeah, please. I have to know how many of my insights were right." He smiled but then started to speak more seriously. "I do hope it goes okay with her. Look…let me give you my number in case you want to talk more. How about you ring me tomorrow and let me know how you got on?"

Tim started scrabbling through his pockets for a piece of paper. He found an old bus ticket and scribbled his mobile phone number on the back.

"Here you go Gemma. Promise you'll call?" He handed her the ticket as she reached the door.

"I will Tim. Thanks again for everything…Um…See ya!"

Gemma left the coffee shop and didn't even notice that it was raining. It had been quite a day. She felt high. Talking with Tim had been amazing and she couldn't quite believe that he wanted her to call him. She didn't think she'd ever felt this happy and was certain that nothing could break her mood.

16
Tests

Melissa walked down the corridor away from the Coronary Care Ward. Her legs felt very shaky. She was sweating and waves of nausea kept overtaking her. The hour that she'd spent with her Dad had felt like a year. Feelings of panic had hit her as soon as she'd walked through the hospital doors and smelt the antiseptic. When she asked for directions to her Dad's ward, her voice shook and she felt close to tears. Why was it suddenly so hard for her to visit a hospital? She couldn't understand the dramatic changes in herself. What was it that she was so afraid of?

Entering the ward had been the hardest part of all. The quiet but rhythmic bleeps from all the heart monitors made her feel ill. The panic she felt was reaching a frightening level. Her heart was racing so fast, she thought she was going to have a heart attack herself. She had finally decided that she really couldn't cope and was about to leave, when she saw her Dad waving and calling out to her. He looked so vulnerable and old in the hospital bed and she knew that she couldn't desert him. She forced herself to walk further into the ward, holding out her card and present in front of her.

"Hey it's my little Melly. All dressed up as if she's going to a funeral." Graham March smiled cheekily at his daughter. "I'm not dead yet love."

"Oh Dad! You know I always wear black. It's supposed to be slimming. Here...open your present," Melissa said as she handed over her gift.

"What's this huh? Chocolates maybe? Some biscuits or ice cream possibly? I'm desperate for some real food."

He looked excitedly into the brown paper bag and pulled out a banana. The disappointment on his face was obvious.

"Oh…fruit. Thank you Melly. It's just what I wanted."

Melissa giggled quietly. She could understand her Dad's disappointment. Chocolate was one of the greatest pleasures in her life too. His health was now telling him that he had to give it up and it didn't look like it was going to be easy for him.

As Melissa told her Dad about her day at school, she found her eyes wandering around the ward. It was hard to focus on her Dad when all she could hear were the persistent heart monitors. Their sound seemed to be amplified in her head. She was terrified that any of the regular bleeps would stop. How would she cope if the alarms went off?

"Did you hear what I said Melly?…Melissa? Are you okay?" Mr. March looked with concern at his daughter.

"Dad?" Melissa asked quietly. "Have you ever seen anyone die?"

"Whoa that's a bit of a gruesome question Melly love. Erm…yeah. I'm afraid I have and in the last 24 hours too. When people come into this ward, they're usually seriously ill and some of them will die. The guy two beds across from me was very poorly when they brought him in. He never regained consciousness and his heart stopped during the night."

Melissa visibly shuddered. The thought of death frightened her so much.

"Dad promise me you will stick to your new diet. I don't want you to die like that other man. PLEASE promise me?"

Mr. March looked at his daughter's intensely serious face.

"Melissa, it's going to be okay you know. You don't have to worry about me. They think that my chest pains were just the result of too much stress. Yes, I'll start eating more healthily. I know I'm overweight and my cholesterol level's too high but you don't need to worry. They'll probably let me go home tomorrow and then I'll have to cope with all your Mum's fussing. So until then, I'm going to make the most of the peace and quiet here."

"This was a warning though Dad and you mustn't ignore it. Right?" For once, Melissa didn't want to joke along with her father. This was a serious matter.

"I'll be fine with you and your Mum to look after me," he replied, beginning to sound slightly fed up with Melissa's persistent questioning. Changing the subject, he continued. "Shall I call a nurse over so that you can ask some questions? It must only be a couple of years now until you start your own nursing training."

Melissa's heart skipped a beat. Talking to a nurse was the last thing she wanted to do. She hadn't told her parents yet that she'd changed her mind about nursing. They had always been so proud of the fact that she'd known what she wanted to be since she was five years old. How was she ever going to tell them that fear had ended her dream? She needed some time and space to think. She had to leave the hospital.

"No Dad. Don't bother a nurse. They're all so busy. I need to get going anyway. I've got heaps of homework to do."

Melissa gave her Dad a final hug and shakily left the hospital. She needed fresh air and found herself taking huge gasping breaths as soon as she was outside. As the panic and sickness started to pass, she was filled with hatred for herself. How could she be so weak and cowardly? She was such a baby and a total failure for being so afraid of the hospital.

She continued to walk slowly down the road. She felt very miserable and realised she had a sudden need for food. It wasn't the solution to her problems but for a while it would take away the pain. Her Mum had once suggested that she might be eating for comfort. Maybe she was right. Certainly Melissa knew that she turned to food whenever she felt sad, angry or fed-up but she hated having those feelings and the food always helped her to get rid of them. When she started to eat, the feelings began to pass. It was as if the food actually squashed them down inside of her.

By this time, she had reached town and saw the burger bar. Her mouth began to water when she thought about the thick milkshakes, golden fries, crispy onion rings and succulent mile high burgers. She forgot the talk she'd had with Gemma about starting a new healthy eating regime and didn't even consider how depressed she became after she'd eaten too much. All she could think about was how desperate she was to eat and which food she should buy.

Five minutes later, she was racing through the park looking for a quiet spot where she could be alone. She was desperate to eat the food that was hidden in her bag and as she ran, she started forcing handfuls of chips into her mouth.

Suddenly she stopped and gaped in horror, her mouth full of half chewed chips. There standing in front of her was Cassie surrounded by a group of her friends. Melissa started to take slow steps backwards. She just couldn't cope with any cruel comments this evening. Her mind was already racing with thoughts of her Dad and the hospital, and a confrontation with Caz would be the final straw. She continued to walk backwards and was just about to turn and run when she heard a shout.

"Look Caz! It's Melissa March and guess what? I think she's eating again!"

As one, the crowd started to run towards Melissa and in no time she found herself pinned against the park gates.

"What you got in your bag Marchers?" Cassie sneered. "I think you owe me after the way you treated me this morning. That was way out of line. Wasn't it girls?"

All of Cassie's crowd started nodding their heads and mumbling their agreement.

"Hand it over then Mellykins. Don't try pretending you don't have any food. I can smell the burger from here and there's grease smeared all round your podgy little face. Grab her bag girls."

Melissa felt her bulging school bag pulled from her shoulder and watched as her precious meal was discovered. Within minutes, the packets and containers were empty as Cassie and her friends gobbled down the greasy food.

"You do realise that we're actually doing you a favour," Cassie muttered, her mouth stuffed with onion rings. "You really shouldn't eat this kind of junk food. It just isn't good for your waistline but then you don't have a waistline do you fatso? Don't you even try to diet? If I were you, I'd feel so ashamed of myself I wouldn't even be able to leave the house. I just don't understand how anyone could let themselves get so massive. What do you think girls?"

Melissa's heart felt heavy. It was bad enough that Cassie stole all her food but her vicious questions were just too much today. They were the same ones that Melissa repeated to herself every day and for which she had no answers. She was fat. A truly revolting person. Why didn't she have any will power? Why couldn't she be more like Gemma? If she wasn't so gross then Cassie wouldn't pick on her. It really was all her own fault wasn't it? Who did she have to blame but herself?

Cassie's comments started to fade as Melissa's head was filled with her own hateful thoughts. She couldn't think of anything good about herself and for the first time ever, the idea of killing herself crossed her mind. What did she have to live for any longer? Her plans for the future now just terrified her. She felt ugly and fat, and no one seemed to like her except maybe Gemma. What was the point?

In the middle of her despairing thoughts, Melissa stopped. Gemma? Why had she thought of Gemma? She'd only really known her for a few days but already she felt there was a bond between them. Gemma had understood and accepted her when she had talked about how difficult dieting was for her. She suddenly realised that she wanted to talk with Gemma again. She wanted to share more of her thoughts and feelings because maybe Gemma would understand and be able to help.

Melissa decided to talk to Gemma as soon as she got to school the next day. It felt so good that for the first time in years, she had a friend to talk to. Looking up, she realised that Cassie and her friends had disappeared. Her bag lay open on the grass and the empty wrappers were discarded all around her. She knelt down and picked up the rubbish. Three chips remained at the bottom of the carton and she quickly ate them. Even the slice of gherkin that Cassie had pushed from the burger seemed appealing. As she chewed on the leftover food and sipped at the few last drops of the milkshake, Melissa decided that she had to ask for help. Food couldn't be the solution to all her problems forever. It wasn't a good solution anyway because after she'd eaten, she always felt guilty and hated herself for being greedy. Maybe Gemma would know what to do…

∞∞∞∞

Across town, Gemma was having serious problems of her own. She'd arrived home to find her Mum in a furious mood. Miss Evans had passed on the news about Gemma's detention and Mrs. Williams was not impressed.

"How could you show me up like that Gemma? I'm the headteacher of your school, something you seem to have forgotten. If you end up in detention, it makes me look like a failure. And that's not fair Gemma because it's not me who's the failure here is it? I'm the one who works hard and succeeds but what have you ever succeeded at? You don't do anything well. You nearly manage this and you nearly manage that but you're just not good enough are you? Oh, I can't even bear to even look at you right now. I'd just get out of my sight if I were you Gemma. You're a disgrace to this family. I'm only glad that your father doesn't have to see what a mess you're making of your life."

Clare Williams knew she was saying too much but her anger was uncontrollable. The shame and embarrassment she'd felt when Miss Evans explained that Gemma was being kept in detention had been overwhelming. She knew that she should talk quietly with Gemma and find out why she'd been given the punishment but she couldn't. All she wanted to do was shout and scream. Her anger needed to be voiced and so she had waited, fuming, until Gemma had returned home.

Gemma heard her mother's words and her bubble of happiness burst. Her head filled with the tormenting words as she struggled to hold back her tears. Her mother was right. She was a failure. Tim was only being kind to her this afternoon. No one could ever really like her. She was something that people pitied. Just like a stray dog.

Banished to her room, Gemma's mood began to change and she started to feel very angry. Why did her mother never listen to her side of the story? And why did she always make everything a competition? Why couldn't she just accept her daughter for who she was? Why did she need her to be top of every class? The more Gemma thought, the angrier she became. And the angrier she became, the guiltier she felt. Anger was an emotion she hated. It wasn't right to get angry was it? People acted badly when they were mad. Her Mum certainly did. She decided she would start exercising. Maybe that would block out the bad feelings she was experiencing. She shouldn't be this angry and she was a horrible person for judging her Mum.

Gemma exercised for over an hour but her feelings of fury just wouldn't subside. She tried to do her homework but she couldn't concentrate. She wanted to call Katee but the phone was in the kitchen and her Mum had made it very clear that she didn't want to see Gemma again that night. She also wanted to chat with Melissa. She needed to talk honestly with someone who understood. Never before had she trusted anyone with her feelings about her Mum.

A feeling of complete hopelessness swept through Gemma. She felt alone and very sad. What was the point in trying any longer? No matter what she did, she could never please her mother. Why had she even bothered to talk with Tim? He'd never want to see her again. Her life was such a mess.

Almost as if a switch had been flipped in her brain, Gemma started to think about food. Suddenly, all she wanted to do was eat. Her feelings of loneliness and sadness began to disappear and her mind was filled with thoughts of food instead. She began to imagine everything that she wanted to eat. Thoughts of chocolate, cakes, crisps, chips and cheese began to fill her mind as she dreamt of all the food that she no longer allowed herself. She imagined walking around a supermarket, choosing whatever she wanted without worrying about the calorie content. Thoughts of ice cream and doughnuts started to make her tastebuds tingle and she knew she had to eat something.

Gemma looked at her watch. It was one o' clock in the morning. Her mother had gone to bed hours ago so the kitchen would finally be empty. Quickly and quietly, she left her room and crept down the stairs. Afraid to turn on a light in case it disturbed her mother, Gemma started to search through the food cupboard by torchlight. She grabbed a packet of chocolate cookies and some bags of crisps. Looking in the fridge, she found cream cakes and mini cheeses. Finally, she opened the freezer and pulled out a large container of ice cream. She felt herself shiver with anticipation and excitement. She knew that the feelings of guilt would engulf her after the binge but nothing could stop her from eating now.

She crept back to her room and quietly closed the door. Starting slowly, Gemma took a single bite from a chocolate éclair. Cream was forced out the sides as her teeth bit into the delicate pastry. As the incredible taste filled her mouth, all the pain and loneliness she felt seemed to vanish. Nothing mattered any more except the food in front of her. Her next bite was bigger than the first. She'd barely swallowed it before she crammed the rest of the cake into her mouth. Reaching for the cookies, she started to tear open the packet. She pushed two of the chocolate biscuits into her mouth while she ripped the lid off the ice cream tub. Using a cookie as a spoon, she started to dig into the melting creamy mixture.

The more Gemma ate, the more she needed to eat and within minutes, all the packets were empty. Even though her stomach was so full that it hurt, Gemma had to have more. She searched desperately through the packets for that one last cookie or crisp. Tears of frustration started to course down her face. She knew she shouldn't eat any more but she couldn't stop so back she went to the kitchen. Grabbing packets of sweets and biscuits, she began eating while she searched for even more food.

Half an hour later, back in her room, Gemma could finally eat no more. She looked around and saw the aftermath of her binge. The guilt hit instantly and was more than she could bear. She started to hit her bloated stomach in disgust and knew she had to make herself sick. Her earlier promises quickly forgotten, she slipped back down the stairs to the little cloakroom. It was as far away from her mother's bedroom as possible and she was certain she couldn't be heard.

Within ten minutes, Gemma was in her room again. She felt dizzy and ill. Her forehead was clammy to the touch and she was exhausted. What had she done to herself? What was the matter with her? She knew that eating so much was wrong but it was as if she were possessed. She had no control when the feelings hit. She had to have food and she had to eat everything that she could find. Sitting on the floor, Gemma started to clear up the mess of crumpled wrappers and crumbs. Her mother mustn't find any evidence of her behaviour, so she started to pack the rubbish into the bottom of her rucksack. She'd throw it away when she walked to school the next day.

When she'd finally tidied her room, Gemma curled up in her bed exhausted. The hatred and disgust she felt for herself was overpowering. She wanted to sleep but the thoughts wouldn't stop racing through her head. After half an hour of tossing and turning, she switched on her bedside lamp and reached down for a book. She lifted up the first book she found and realised it was the one about eating disorders. Oh well.

At least she could do some good and learn more about anorexia so that she could try and help Katee.

As she flicked through the chapters, Gemma found herself astonished by how complicated eating disorders really were. She was horrified as she read about the dangers of anorexia and learnt what happened to the body if you didn't feed it properly. Her greatest shock of all though came when she found a chapter about bulimia. She almost didn't continue reading because the introduction didn't seem to relate to Katee at all but then a sentence caught her eye.

"Quite often, feelings of hunger or difficult emotions cause bulimics to binge on large quantities of food they so desperately want."

Gemma sat up in bed. She was suddenly aware that she was now reading about herself. She felt scared and there was a part of her that was desperate to close the book so that she couldn't learn anything more. She wanted to pretend that there was nothing wrong at all. However, there was another part of her that had to know more.

"Following a binge, bulimics usually suffer tremendous guilt as well as physical pain from the large amount of food they have eaten. This guilt leads the sufferer to find ways to get rid of the food. Self-induced vomiting is common."

Gemma's heart was pounding. Was she bulimic? She binged and vomited. Did that mean she had bulimia? Surely not. She only did it occasionally so that couldn't be harmful could it? She wanted to stop reading but she had to learn if her behaviour was dangerous. Her hands were shaking so much that she could barely turn the pages but she needed the reassurance. She had to discover that she was not hurting herself. Finally, she managed to turn the page. The words she read did not calm her nerves but instead filled her with a chilling fear.

"...Vomiting puts bulimics at risk of a heart attack at any time...Epileptic fits can happen...Teeth are ruined by vomiting...Some bulimics suffer massive internal bleeds that can lead to death... "

The book slipped from Gemma's shaking hands. What if there was even just a chance that these terrible things could happen to her? If she had a heart attack, people would find out that she made herself sick. The shame of that would be terrible. Gemma turned out the light and slid down in her bed. Her eyes stung from crying and her heart was still pounding. She had to think but her mind just wouldn't focus. She needed help. She couldn't cope alone any longer. She had to share her feelings and troubles with someone. She would try talking with Melissa. Maybe she'd know what to do.

17
The Crisis

Katee looked around the waiting room in amazement. Everyone else there was over the age of sixty. She felt like a freak. Why did she need an ECG? She wasn't going to have a heart attack. The doctor was crazy. She wanted to ask her Mum why they were doing these tests but she felt it was her mother's fault that she was there and so was deliberately staying silent.

The night before had been a nightmare. When they'd returned home, her Mum had tried to calmly explain the situation to her Dad. He didn't seem to understand though and even through her thick bedroom door, she had heard his angry words. He wouldn't accept that his daughter was ill and kept repeating that the doctor was being ridiculous. He was certain that Katee was just a difficult teenager and all they needed to do was be a lot stricter with her. No more eating in her room. No more excuses to avoid meals. She would have to join them at the table just like her brother David always did. They were going to eat together as a family from now on. Jane had tried very hard to explain that their daughter needed gentle understanding but Brian Quinn simply wasn't listening. These days his answer to every problem just seemed to be harshness. His caring nature appeared to have vanished overnight. There were times when Jane couldn't even accept that this was the man she married. What had happened lately? Why had he changed so much?

The evening meal had been an horrendous event for everyone. Brian had insisted that Katee ate a full plate of food and had even served up her dinner himself. Katee's expression was one of blind panic when she saw the amount that she was expected to eat. That was when the fight really began. Their quiet, studious daughter seemed to change before their very eyes. Anger had flooded Katee's body again and she'd started shouting.

"You really hate me don't you? You must if you expect me to eat all that food! There's no way I'm doing that! You can lock me in my room or yell at me or even hit me," Katee looked defiantly at her Dad. "But I'm not going to eat anything! You just want to make me fat don't you? Why won't you just leave me alone?"

Then Katee shocked everyone into silence. She picked up her plate, which was loaded with shepherds pie and vegetables, and threw it at the wall. The whole family watched as huge lumps of gravy covered potato slowly slid down the patterned wallpaper onto the floor. Horrified by what she'd done, Katee gazed in amazement at the growing mess on the carpet.

The first slap took her by complete surprise and she stared open mouthed at her father. The second slap stung badly and instinctively

Katee put her hands over her face and started to back away. As he saw her cower, Brian's anger grew even stronger and he reached forward to hit his daughter a third time. David couldn't believe the scene unfolding before him. He loved both his sister and his father. Why were they behaving like this? Grabbing his Dad's arm, he started yelling.

"Dad what are you doing? You can't do that! You can't hurt Katee like that! Are you mad? You mustn't hit her! DAD! STOP!! PLEASE!!!" David's voice grew louder with every word he spoke.

The protests gradually started to register in Brian's head as he slowly pulled his arm free of his son's grip. Anger still showed in his face though and through gritted teeth, he hissed at his young daughter.

"Go to your room you disgusting piece of garbage! You make me sick! You're just a spoilt ungrateful brat and things are going to change around here from now on! There'll be no more of your petty temper tantrums. You will do what I say or else there'll be trouble. Do you hear me? DO YOU HEAR ME?"

Katee was shaking uncontrollably and tears were pouring down her face. Slowly she nodded her head. She tried to speak but no words would come out of her mouth. She wasn't sure which frightened her more. The angry man in front of her that she called her father or the strong feelings inside herself that were so powerful and controlled her actions. Without even looking at anyone, she ran from the room. She had to be alone.

Jane Quinn looked at her husband. She felt confusion and disbelief. What was happening? Brian had just hit their daughter. Twice. It had happened so fast that she hadn't even been able to stop him. If David hadn't been in the room who knows what would have happened? Would Brian have continued to beat Katee? Had he ever done it before when no one else was around? So many questions filled her head. She needed time to think about everything she'd just seen. She needed to work out how she felt about Brian. Could she really love a man who could beat his own daughter and then shout such cruel words at her? She also needed to talk with Katee. She needed to tell her that she loved her and cared about her.

Brian stomped angrily out of the house and Jane looked at the mess. Before she even started to clean up, she knew that she had to talk to her daughter. When she walked into Katee's bedroom, a very strange sight greeted her. Her daughter was gazing transfixed at a large, sharp needle which she was holding in her hand. Jane asked her what she was doing and Katee murmured that she had split her skirt that day and needed to stitch it up. At first Jane believed her but then she saw blood on a tissue and her heart started to race. What was happening to the girl she had once known so well? Had Katee been cutting herself? Jane tried to ignore the tissue and started to apologise.

"Katee love, I'm so sorry about what happened tonight. I really don't know what got into your father. I think he was quite shocked by what the doctor said and just didn't want to accept that there might be a problem. Please honey…please accept our apologies. I'll try and make your father understand. I think I should take him along to the surgery so that Dr. Morgan can explain the situation to him. It won't always be like this love. Meals can be a happy time again."

The silence that greeted Jane was deafening. Katee was staring into space, almost as if she was in shock. A lone drop of blood ran down her hand and onto the bedcover. Jane stared transfixed.

"Katee! Darling! You're bleeding! Look at your arm! What have you done?"

Katee slowly looked down at her lap. She couldn't understand her mother's concern. She didn't feel the scratches. Shock was dulling the pain. In a voice totally devoid of emotion, she spoke quietly to her.

"Oh it's nothing Mum. I just slipped when I was stitching my skirt."

"Please let me look at your arm love. Let me see the cut." Jane's voice was low and gentle but Katee started to move away from her into the corner of the room.

"NO!" she yelled.

The sudden shout echoed around the room and Jane saw the terror in her daughter's face. Gently trying to pacify the young girl, Jane spoke in whispers.

"It's okay honey, I won't touch your arm. Come back onto the bed and sit down. You look so tired. Here, let me put that needle away for you." Jane took the needle and carefully put it back in Katee's sewing box before continuing. "Why don't you get into your pyjamas and I'll go downstairs and get you a hot drink? It's been such a bad evening for you. You need some pampering."

"Just black coffee Mum. The milk makes me sick." The words were out of Katee's mouth before she could stop them. It was almost as if the anorexia spoke for her now. The truth was that she really wanted a large mug of steaming cocoa and a heap of chocolate cookies but she could never allow herself such a treat. She didn't deserve any food. She was a bad person. A disgusting piece of garbage and a spoilt ungrateful brat. Her father's words had already begun to echo through her head.

"Okay Katee but wouldn't you like just a little piece of cake? You didn't eat any of your dinner and you know what the doctor said."

"No Mum. No cake."

"Well how about a little salad then love?" Jane suggested hopefully.

"Okay," Katee said finally. "But NO dressing."

Jane sighed and quietly left the room. It was evident that Katee's problem with food was worse than she'd originally thought and what on earth had she been doing with that needle? Again, the questions began to race through her mind. As a mother, what had she done wrong? Weren't eating disorders always the fault of the parents? She felt a failure and the guilt was tremendous. Perhaps there would be a doctor at the hospital tomorrow who she could talk with.

∞∞∞∞

Sitting next to her daughter in the hospital waiting room the following morning, Jane was finding it hard to accept what had happened the night before. It felt like a dream until she looked across at Katee. The teenager was hunched in her seat with her head bowed. Her once tight uniform now hung loosely on her skinny frame. Her face was ghostly pale and there were deep black shadows under her eyes. Jane struggled to keep her emotions in check. What was the doctor going to find when he monitored her heart? Had some damage already been done?

"Katee Quinn to Room 14 for Doctor Elliot."

Jane heard the nurse and saw Katee stand up. All of a sudden, she felt a fierce desire to protect her child and wanted to bundle this thin girl up in her arms and race her away from the hospital. It felt almost unbearable to think that she could no longer save her child from the pain and fear of the hospital tests.

"Do you want me to come with you Katee?" she offered.

It was a cold emotionless voice that replied.

"No Mum. I'll go alone. You've done enough already. I don't want you telling this doctor lies as well."

Jane knew how alone and upset her child was. The anger she showed was understandable but her words still hurt. She bit hard on her lip and silently nodded at her daughter, trying to give a final reassuring smile. When she saw Katee disappear down the corridor, she walked over to the reception desk.

"Hello…um… my name's Mrs. Quinn. Katee's Mum and I was…er…just wondering if you could tell me whether there was any chance that I could speak with Dr. Elliot at all this morning?"

The receptionist looked up from her pile of notes and appointment cards in frustration. Reassuring distressed parents really wasn't part of her job. She was just there to book in patients and send out new appointment times. She was about to launch into her usual speech, explaining that it was the duty nurse who would be able to help, when she saw the concern on Jane's face.

"Well it isn't really my job Mrs. Quinn but I'll see what I can do. Leave it with me and I'll call you if I can arrange something."

Jane sat back in her seat with relief and looked across at the locked door of Room 14. She wondered how Katee was coping.

∞∞∞∞

Dr. Elliot was waiting for Katee in Room 14 with an encouraging smile on his face. From first impressions, he appeared to be quite pleasant but Katee didn't care. She wanted to hate him anyway. As she walked into the small clinic, he began talking and introduced the nurse who was standing by the sink. Then he asked Katee to climb up onto the hard couch that ran along the side wall. It was covered by a long blue sheet of paper and Katee slid sideways as she tried to scramble on.

"Okay Katee, let me explain what we're going to do today," Dr. Elliot said cheerily. "Your doctor has asked us to take some blood so that we can do a range of tests. We need to discover what your electrolyte levels are like and also to check your blood cell count to see if you're anaemic. Have you had a blood test before?"

For the first time since she'd arrived in the room, Katee slowly lifted her head and found herself looking into the doctor's sympathetic blue eyes. She wanted to hate this man. The 'voice' had told her that she had to hate him. She was supposed to be as uncooperative as possible but her guard was starting to slip. How could she hate someone with such a friendly face? She realised that she had to be strong though or else the anorexic 'voice' would punish her later. Pinching her thigh, she felt the sharp pain and her expression changed to show nothing but unhappiness.

"Yes. I've had one once," she said moodily.

"Right well then I don't really have to explain it all to you. What I will need you to do though is to roll up the sleeve on your left arm."

Katee stared at the doctor in disbelief. Why hadn't it even occurred to her that they would need to see her arm? Pulling her jumper down firmly over her scratched forearm, she began to shake her head.

"No I can't do that. You can't take blood from that arm."

"Why's that Katee?" the doctor queried.

"Because you just can't okay? You can only use my right arm coz I er…I…hit my left arm in hockey yesterday and it's badly bruised and swollen."

"Oh I'm sorry about that. Do you want me to have a look at it to check that it's not broken or sprained?"

"No, it's fine honest. Just bruised but I…er…I don't want you to take any blood from it."

"Okay, that's not a worry. We can use your right arm just as easily. If you'll just roll your sleeve up for me then."

Katee breathed out with relief and quickly rolled up her sleeve. That had been a close call. It was amazing how often she found herself lying these days. She always seemed to find an excuse though, even for the toughest problems. It was like the 'voice' was teaching her how to lie. She barely felt the prick of the needle as the doctor drew the blood but she still couldn't watch him. It was just too ghoulish to see her own blood filling the vials.

When the doctor had finished, Katee rolled down her sleeve and started to get up from the couch.

"No, stay up there Katee. We still need to do the ECG. Now before we do this, let me explain a little more about exactly what the procedure is. ECG stands for Electrocardiogram and it's a machine that records the electrical activity in your heart. We're going to attach some electrodes to the surface of your chest and then the electrical pulses will be recorded as waves on paper. By studying these waves, we can see if you have an irregularities in your heart beat. The procedure is painless and it only takes a few minutes but I will need you to take off your shirt and jumper for me so that I can stick on the electrodes. While the nurse is helping you with your clothes, I'll just warm up these electrodes so that you don't get a shock."

"But I can't!" Katee replied loudly.

"Sorry Katee. You can't what?"

"I can't take off my clothes."

"Oh. Because of your sore arm? That's okay. The nurse will help."

"No I just can't take them off."

How would the 'voice' help her get out of this?

"Katee, I know it feels a bit embarrassing but I promise you there's nothing to worry about. The test will be really quick and in just five minutes we'll be all done. Nurse? Can you help Katee with her clothes?"

Katee realised that she had very little choice. She could get angry like she did the night before but what was the point? They were going to do the test one way or another. She realised that she'd finally been defeated and the 'voice' would punish her for failing.

Why hadn't it helped her?

Slowly, she started to remove her clothes until she was wearing nothing but her small crop top.

Dr. Elliot looked down at the angry red scratch marks on Katee's thin left arm and instantly knew why she'd been so reluctant to remove her clothes. There was obviously a lot of pain in this young girl's life if she had started to self-harm. He knew that she expected him to comment on her cuts but instead he just smiled kindly and asked her to relax back onto the couch.

Katee shuddered as each of the electrodes was attached to her body. Three times they fell off because they had difficulty sticking to her bony chest. Dr. Elliot had to run the test three times because Katee was shaking so fiercely for the first ten minutes. Eventually, he told her a funny story about his old dog and gradually she calmed down enough for him to get a proper reading.

With the test finally completed, Katee was allowed to get dressed. Dr. Elliot sat down in front of her and started to talk.

"I've completed the tests that your doctor asked for Katee and we will be sending the results through to him in the next few days. He'll probably contact you as soon as they're through. Is there anything that you want to ask me before you leave? Any questions at all?"

Katee looked thoughtfully at the caring young doctor. She wanted to know what they would do if any of the tests came back with negative results but she just couldn't ask the question. It was too frightening to even think of the possibility that something was really wrong. Besides, the 'voice' told her that she was fine and that they were all making a fuss about nothing.

"No thank you," she replied quietly.

"Okay Katee," Dr. Elliot said, reaching out to shake her hand. "It was really nice meeting you this morning. You know the way back to the waiting room don't you?"

Katee nodded and walked towards the door. Part of her desperately wanted to tell this doctor how unhappy she really felt and ask for his help but that wasn't part of the 'voice's plan.

Dr. Elliot watched the slight figure disappear down the corridor into the waiting room. He made a mental note to write to her doctor about the self-harming. Katee Quinn needed some help and he wanted to recommend a therapist at the hospital called Sally Wilkins, who'd had a lot of success with anorexia nervosa.

18
Sharing Secrets

The day did not start well for Gemma. She had arrived downstairs in time for breakfast only to be met with another lecture. Her mother had discovered an empty cookie packet on the kitchen floor and she was not pleased.

"If you're going to have midnight feasts Gemma then at least try and eat something healthier. Cookies aren't going to give you all the vitamins and minerals that you need to stay fit and well."

Gemma had felt instantly sick when she'd seen the empty wrapper. She'd been so certain that she hadn't left any signs of her early morning binge. Had her mother found any other evidence in the cupboard or fridge? Gemma tried to think of a plausible excuse but she couldn't find the words to explain away the empty packet. However, Mrs. Williams hadn't even noticed Gemma's silence and just continued talking.

"You have to be more responsible Gemma. This is exactly what I was talking about last night. You can't expect everyone else to look after you forever. Do you understand that?"

Gemma remembered nodding at her mother, who then appeared to make an effort to change her mood.

"Okay Gemma, well I think I've said enough. Please remember though, NO MORE detentions. I've packed you a healthy lunch and I'll see you this evening. Let me know if you're going to be late okay?"

Mrs. Williams gave her daughter a stilted smile and a formal hug. Gemma knew her mother was trying hard to put the previous evening behind them but why could she never actually apologise? She really could not understand her mother's problem. She herself never had any difficulty saying sorry if she felt she'd made a mistake. Maybe the truth was that her Mum never actually believed she'd done anything wrong. Maybe she really did think it was right to expect so much from her daughter. Gemma realised again that she needed to talk with Melissa. She felt so confused. Was she wrong to be this upset by her mother's behaviour? She packed her bag and grabbing her lunch, left the house. She was nervous about talking honestly with Melissa but there was an underlying feeling of relief that she wouldn't be alone with her problems any longer.

∞∞∞∞

Gemma wasn't able to meet up with Melissa until the third period and by then, she was having doubts. She wondered if she really should share her worries. Maybe she was just making a fuss about nothing. After all, she did only make herself sick occasionally. And everyone had problems with their parents didn't they? She had finally convinced herself not to say a word when Melissa came rushing up to her, her face alive with excitement.

"Gemma Hi. I've been searching for you all morning. I've got so much I want to talk to you about. I was in the park yesterday and Cassie and her whole gang were picking on me again and I realised so many different things. Would it be okay if I…well if I…um…talked to you about some stuff?"

Forgetting the promise she'd made to herself only moments earlier, Gemma smiled broadly and started talking excitedly herself.

"Wow, this is amazing Melissa. Loads of things happened to me last night too and I decided that I really needed to talk to you. Look, let's go and find somewhere quiet so that we can talk."

The two girls both had a free period before their Maths lesson so they found an empty classroom and hurriedly sat down. They looked at each other shyly and giggled.

"Well?" said Gemma. "You first."

"Noooo. After you Gemma please," Melissa replied.

The two girls giggled and debated for a few minutes until Melissa finally found the courage to start telling her story.

"Okay okay. I'll be the brave one and go first." Gradually, Melissa told Gemma all about the night before, starting with her trip to the hospital and ending with her realisations in the park.

"I felt so disgusting Gemma, crawling about on the ground searching for the bits of food that Cassie left behind. But I just couldn't stop myself. I knew how sad I must have looked but I desperately needed that food." Melissa paused, as if she was trying to find the courage to say something else.

"Now this is going to sound totally mad but it's like by stuffing down food I can make some of my feelings disappear. When I'm eating, nothing else matters except the food although – and this is gonna sound like the weirdest thing of all – after about five minutes I can't actually taste what I'm eating any more. Even that doesn't stop me though. I just keep forcing food into my mouth. You know it's like I've lost the ability to stop. I feel really full but I just keep eating and eating and that makes me feel so disgusted with myself. I just end up thinking that I'm so vile and I really hate myself. Every time I look at my body or someone teases me for being fat, I just remember how greedy and revolting I am."

Melissa came to a sudden stop. She hadn't expected to say so much but when she began speaking, the words had just tumbled out. After a while she hadn't even felt able to look at Gemma and had begun talking to a small spot on the floor. Finally, she forced herself to look at her friend. She was convinced that Gemma would be revolted but the look on her face certainly wasn't one of disgust. It looked as though she really understood and what she said next only confirmed this.

"Omigod Melissa. I understand your feelings so well because… er…well…because I do the same thing."

"What?" Melissa couldn't believe what she was hearing. "Look Gemma I've been honest with you. Don't make fun of me. You can't do the same as me because if you did then you'd be…well you'd be as fat as I am."

"No Mel, I'm not making fun of you. I really do exactly the same thing as you and for exactly the same reason. To push away my feelings. But… I do something else too that's really disgusting. I think that when I tell you about it, you probably won't want anything more to do with me but…but I have to tell someone because I'm scared and I just don't know what to do."

Gemma took a deep breath as she tried to prepare herself to talk about her secret. Melissa watched her friend silently. She couldn't quite understand what Gemma was talking about but knew that she should just wait patiently.

"Okay. I guess the best way to say this is to just blurt it all out," Gemma finally said. "If you hate me after I've told you, that's okay. I'll understand. Don't feel that you have to pretend you still want to be friends…Urgh! This is so hard." Gemma stared at Melissa and took another deep breath. "Okay. Well the reason I'm not larger is because I…well it's because I don't… it's because I make myself sick after I've binged."

Gemma's face flooded with colour. She felt so ashamed and couldn't bear to look at Melissa's face. She heard the screech of a chair moving and her heart sunk. Melissa must have been so disgusted that she couldn't even stay in the same room. She nearly jumped out of her skin when Melissa took her hand and gently spoke.

"Thanks for talking about it, Gemma. No one's ever really trusted me like that before. Can you tell me a bit more? Do you do it much? Isn't it dangerous? I mean I don't really know much about it except that I did try to make myself sick once. I'd eaten so much and my stomach really hurt and I felt disgusting and I was so desperate to get rid of the food but I just couldn't do it. I tried twice but I was too scared. I just really hate being sick."

"I'm glad you couldn't do it Mel. I found out last night that it's really dangerous. I was reading this book about eating disorders so that I could maybe help Katee more and I started reading this page about bulimia. And it was me. It was all about me. I was terrified because vomiting is so dangerous. Do you know that I could have had a heart attack while I was making myself sick? This book said that it upsets your…erm…your…hang on."

Rifling through her bag, Gemma grabbed the book she'd borrowed from the library. At the same time, she caught sight of all the empty packets and wrappers from the previous night. Before she could stop and think, she began pulling out the evidence of her binge.

"Look Melissa. This is what I ate last night. All this food and then I made myself sick. That's why I understand how you feel. I was full of so much anger and sadness and frustration last night and I got this feeling like I just had to eat. Then, when I'd eaten, I felt so guilty and so bloated that I had no choice. I had to throw up. But I can't do that again Mel. I need help. I don't want to die from this." Gemma stopped and gave a hollow laugh. "Whoa! That sounds so dramatic doesn't it but this book...it just petrified me."

Gemma started flicking quickly through the book.

"Look here. It says that if you binge and vomit then you really upset your...electrolyte balance and that can cause heart problems."

Gemma suddenly felt that she was close to tears and fell silent so that she could compose herself again. Melissa looked at her with concern. This all felt so unreal. She'd had no idea that Gemma was hiding such a secret. She had always seemed so together – so pretty and with such a lovely figure. Why would she feel a need to binge and then vomit? Before she could work out if it was okay to ask more questions, she realised that she was already speaking.

"Gemma, why do you do it? What are these feelings that you're trying to push away?"

Like a dam bursting, the words began flooding from Gemma. She described her mother's competitive nature and how this had eventually driven her father away.

"When Dad left, Mum got even worse. She just focused all her attention on her career and whatever time she had left over, she spent worrying about my future. I can never do anything right Mel. Sometimes it just drives me crazy. Like last night, when she screamed at me for getting a detention. I mean everyone gets detention from time to time don't they? But she said I was doing it deliberately just to ruin her career. I mean is that paranoid or what? And then she actually had the nerve to tell me that it was lucky Dad wasn't around 'cause he'd be so ashamed of me. Me? It was her that he couldn't live with and I can so understand that."

Gemma felt all the anger forcing its way to the surface again as she told Melissa about her home life.

"You know what felt really unfair about last night Mels?" Melissa shook her head and Gemma continued. "I was actually happy for once. I haven't really felt happy since I moved schools. It's hard to settle in somewhere different and I've felt really out of place since the beginning of term. And then yesterday I met this guy Tim in the library and I also realised that you were a friend and I felt happier than I had in ages but Mum just spoilt it all. The binge started because I just couldn't cope with my feelings any more and I wanted them to go away. It's what you said Mel. It's like the food squashes the feelings down inside you."

The two girls continued to talk about their feelings and the more they shared, the calmer they felt. They both saw how much they had in common and slowly realised that they were no longer alone with their fears and worries. Eventually it was Melissa who asked the most difficult question of all.

"What are we going to do Gemma? We need to change don't we? How are we going to do that? Have you got any ideas?"

"Well…yeah. I did have a few thoughts but they all just seemed too frightening last night."

"Okay," Melissa said calmly. "But we're in this together now. Tell me what they were and maybe we can work something out."

"Right. Well this book suggests that you go and see your doctor to have a check up but I don't know if I can face that yet. I'm really worried that my Mum will find out if I do that. It also said that there are support groups and therapists that can help you to work out why your problems started. What do you think Mel?"

"Hmmmm. Interesting. Well I can understand that you're scared about seeing your doctor. I am too because whenever I do go and see him he always tells me I need to lose weight and that depresses me, which means that I just start eating again. The support group thing sounds like a good idea because we could maybe go together and then it wouldn't be so scary. But how would we find out about a support group?"

"Do you think they have one at the hospital?"

"Maybe." Melissa went quiet for a minute while she thought. "Hey I've got an idea. You could come with me to visit my Dad tonight and we could ask a nurse if there's a group for people with eating problems."

"Whoa! Tonight huh?" Gemma looked shocked. "That soon? It sounds really scary but...I guess it's a good idea isn't it? I really don't want to make myself sick any more but sometimes it just sort of happens and I need to know how to stop it. Okay. Yeah," she said, trying to sound more positive. "I'll come with you tonight and we'll see what happens. I guess I ought to tell my Mum that I'll be late."

The two girls looked at one another. Suddenly Gemma smiled.

"Hey, we've both just taken the first step towards recovery."

"What's that?" Melissa asked, puzzled.

"Well I was reading last night that telling someone you have a problem and asking for help is the first step towards getting better.

It was amazing. We both did it at exactly the same time. Maybe that's a good sign. Maybe we're going to be okay Mel."

"I do hope so Gemma. And maybe because of all this, we'll be able to help Katee more. By the way, do you know if she's okay? She wasn't in class this morning."

19
The Friendship Grows

Jane Quinn tried to encourage Katee to go home and rest for the remainder of the day but her daughter was very determined. She wanted to go back to school and there was nothing Jane could say that would change her mind. Doctor Elliot had advised Jane to make sure her daughter had a cup of tea and some biscuits as soon as possible. The tests had depleted her blood levels and she needed to replenish them before she did anything else. However, Katee would not co-operate with her mother and the two soon fell into another fierce argument. Jane hated shouting at her child but found that she just couldn't help herself. She was so worried. As she'd watched Katee walk out of the clinic, her heart had missed a beat. It was as if she was looking at her daughter for the first time in months and she was horrified by what she saw.

Doctor Elliot had agreed to talk in more depth with her when the test results came through. He had encouraged her to speak with her own family doctor first though as he didn't want to compromise patient confidentiality. This had left Jane feeling even more panicked. She hadn't been able to tell anyone about the sharp needle or the blood she'd seen dripping from Katee's arm the night before. All her frustrations and fears had finally erupted when Katee refused to eat or drink before returning to school that morning.

"Look what you're doing to yourself Katee! You have to eat! You have NO choice! Why are you being so selfish? Don't you know how worried I am about you? You're getting so thin. You look just like a famine victim! It's disgusting!"

Shocked by her own reaction, Jane stopped in her tracks. How could she be talking to her daughter like this? She didn't even recognise herself. She immediately started to apologise but could see the hurt and pain in Katee's eyes. She had caused her daughter even more distress. What kind of a mother was she? The guilt she felt was overwhelming and she realised that she did need to talk to the doctor. She no longer had any idea how to help her own child and it was tearing her apart.

∞∞∞∞∞

Katee walked into the classroom half way through a Maths class. She felt strange. Her head ached and her eyes wouldn't focus properly but she couldn't give up now. Finally she was losing some weight and no one was going to stop her. The 'voice' told her to refuse all food and she wasn't going to disobey it. She just couldn't do that. It was such a powerful force inside of her. The cuts on her arms still throbbed and they were a constant reminder that it was the 'voice' which was really in control.

She apologised to Miss Evans for being late and stumbled to her desk. The room kept spinning and her stomach rumbled loudly. She hadn't eaten for over twenty-five hours and the 'voice' was pleased. The trip to the hospital had been terrible. The 'voice' had been yelling at her ever since the ECG. Undressing in front of the doctor and nurse had been so humiliating. She hated the sight of her own body and had seen nothing but fat bulging out from beneath her crop top. The 'voice' had told her many times already that day just how repulsive she'd looked.

Katee tried to concentrate on the Maths lesson but all she could think about was food. Pressing down on her stomach, she tried to stop the rumbling but people were beginning to notice and she heard some distant giggling. Her face coloured with embarrassment and she tried to cough to cover the noises. She breathed a huge sigh of relief when she finally heard the end of lesson bell.

As the girls gradually left the classroom, Gemma walked over to Katee's desk.

"Hi Katee. It's great to see you back at school today. Here's your diary," she said, handing over the journal. "It must have fallen out of your bag when you fainted. I kept it safe for you. No one's looked in it I swear. So...are you feeling a little better?"

Katee was taken by surprise. She'd been trying to decide whether she could allow herself an apple for lunch. She knew that she had to stop her stomach rumbling but would the 'voice' let her eat anything?

"Oh Gemma! Hi! Erm...er...yeah. Thanks for the book," Katee said, quickly shuffling her precious diary out of sight. "Yeah. I feel a little bit better."

"You still look a bit pale though," Gemma continued. "Would you like to share some of my lunch?"

Katee stared at Gemma in surprise. She had been so rude to her already this week. Why was she still being so friendly? A little smile started to play around her lips. She was very curious to see what Gemma had for lunch. In the last few months she'd found herself peering shyly at other people's meals to see exactly what they ate.

"Well…er…what have you got?"

Gemma was caught a little off guard by Katee's answer. She had expected a sharp "No!" in response. Excitedly, she opened her lunchbox, knocking books off the table in her haste to show Katee her food. Together, they peered into the blue plastic container.

"Well my Mum packed it this morning and told me it was a 'healthy' lunch so it isn't going to be that exciting. Let's see. Um…I have two apples, an orange, some sandwiches, which I think may have some kind of cheese in them, a banana, a yoghurt and a cereal bar. Do you fancy any of that Katee?"

"Well…I wouldn't mind an apple if you can spare it… " Katee said quietly.

Gemma beamed at the other girl.

"Of course I can spare it. I've got enough fruit in here to start a greengrocer's."

Katee snorted with laughter and grabbed one of the apples from the box. Her stomach rumbled with anticipation as she examined the juicy red fruit.

Melissa had sat quietly at the back of the room, watching while Gemma chatted with Katee. She'd been amazed to see Katee smile and even laugh out loud at times as Gemma showed her a lunchbox filled with food. She felt proud of the girl she now called her best friend. The conversation they'd had only an hour before had drawn them even closer and she was glad to see that Gemma was starting to connect with Katee as well. A shout drew her out of her thoughts.

"Hey Melissa! Do you wanna come and join us? I've got enough healthy food in here to feed a team of athletes."

Melissa smiled and walked down to the front of the classroom. This was pretty cool. The three of them sharing a lunch for the first time. She sat down next to Gemma and reached into the lunchbox for a cheese sandwich.

"Hey Gemma, tell Katee about Tim," she said. "I want to know what she thinks 'cause I'm certain you should phone him. He asked you to, so you really should you know."

Gemma blushed and started to explain about her meeting with Tim. She carefully edited the story so that Katee didn't know they'd spent most of their time discussing anorexia and the book on eating disorders. By the time she'd finished her story, Katee was grinning.

"This is so exciting. You've almost got a boyfriend Gemma. Wow! Melissa's right though. You just have to phone him. Do it now. Go on. I can lend you some money if you need it. Go on. Do it now so that you can tell us what he says."

It was wonderful to see the excitement in Katee's face. She had come alive and her eyes were sparkling. A tiny apple core lay on the desk to indicate that Katee had munched her way through the fruit while Gemma told her story. The small number of calories the apple contained and the warmth of friendship had given Katee back some life. Gemma felt she just couldn't disappoint her.

"Okay then. Come on. Let's go down to the phones and I'll give Tim a ring. Omigod. I feel so nervous. It's like my stomach's doing somersaults. Unless that's just 'cause I ate too much of my Mum's high fibre lunch."

The three girls giggled together as they walked down the corridor to the phone booth by the front door. Gemma searched in her bag and found the number Tim had given her the previous evening.

"Okay then…here goes."

Her fingers shook as she dialled the number and she drew a deep breath as the rings began. Counting up to six, she was about to put the phone down when she heard a breathless voice.

"Hello? Tim Rosen speaking."

Gemma froze. She had no idea what to say to the man on the other end of the line. She started to stutter.

"Erm…it's…um…it's…er…me. It's Gemma Williams. We…er…met in a coffee shop yesterday and…er…"

Before she could finish her sentence, Tim interrupted.

"Gemma! It's great to hear from you. I've been hoping all day that you'd call and I haven't let my mobile out of my sight and then I rushed off to the toilet quickly and I heard it ringing and I thought it might be you and I was worried I would miss it and…sorry. I think I'm babbling. How are you?"

"I'm fine. Really fine. Very fine. Oh…er…well maybe not really fine but I'm okay. It's really alright for me to ring you again? I sort of thought that you might have just said I could call out of…I don't know…politeness maybe?"

"Oh no Gemma no! I don't say things just to be kind. I really enjoyed seeing you yesterday. How did it go with Katee?"

Gemma had forgotten that Tim would probably ask about Katee. She knew she had to carefully indicate to him that the girl in question was standing right beside her.

"Well I'm here with Melissa and Katee and they managed to convince me to give you a ring. I was feeling too nervous."

"Ahh I see. We'll talk about it later then, yeah?"

Gemma smiled. It was always so easy to chat with Tim. Her nerves had vanished already and she wanted to talk to him all afternoon. However, she knew her money was running out. Calls to mobile phones were expensive and it wasn't going to be long before they were cut off.

"Yeah, that'd be good. Erm…Tim I…um…haven't got too much money left and I'm going to have to go soon."

"Do you want me to ring you back?"

"I'm ringing from school and they don't allow us to have incoming calls on this phone. Sorry about that."

"Oh okay," Tim said, sounding disappointed. "How about we meet Saturday then? You could pick a movie if you like or we could just go for coffee again."

"Wow. That'd be really fun," Gemma said, trying to contain her excitement. "Yeah I'd like that. Shall I give you another ring on Friday so we can set a time and a place to meet?"

Gemma just heard the words "Yep, that'd be great…" before her money ran out and she was cut off. She hung the phone back on its hook and turned to face the two girls beside her. They couldn't help but smile back at her because of the huge grin on her face.

"Tim asked me on a date!"

Katee and Melissa squealed together in delight until Gemma waved her hands frantically to quieten them.

"Come on. Let's go back to the classroom. If we get caught making this kind of noise out here we'll all get detention. And then my life would seriously be over."

Walking back to the classroom Katee realised that she was smiling. She knew that it wasn't her that had been asked on a date but she felt happy for the first time in months. She felt pleased for Gemma and excited that she was part of a group. Suddenly, she heard the 'voice' begin to speak…

20
The Support Group

When the bell rang for the end of school, Gemma had mixed feelings. She'd spent the afternoon thinking through all the events that had happened that day. Not only had she become a closer friend to Melissa but Katee had shared her lunch too. Then there was the most exciting moment of all, when Tim had asked her out on a date. She'd found herself smiling at everyone all afternoon, even the teachers. However, now she was feeling nervous. She wished she hadn't agreed to Melissa's suggestion about the support group and now wanted to hide her secret away again. The shame she felt about her problems made her believe it would be easier to pretend they didn't exist. She knew that Melissa wouldn't let her back out though and she realised her friend was right. The previous night had shown her that the bulimia could take over at any time without warning. She needed to take a positive step forward. The support group might not be as frightening as she thought and Melissa would be there with her. Taking a deep breath, she tidied her desk and packed her bag. She had promised to meet Melissa by the lockers and she was going to be late if she didn't hurry.

Melissa arrived at the meeting place first and was also feeling nervous. She hadn't wanted to return to the hospital so soon but knew that she had to face her fears. Maybe the support group would help her to understand why she often felt so afraid.

Melissa broke into a broad grin as she saw Gemma hurrying down the corridor, stuffing books into her bag as she ran.

"Sorry I'm late Mel. Our English lesson ran over time. You know what Mrs. Crane's like. She's just won't let you go until she's finished discussing the point she's making. It wasn't even interesting stuff she was saying either. I mean I don't mind too much if we're doing an interesting book but I just can't get into the one we're reading right now. It's so boring. My mind wanders and then I'm in dead schtuck when I'm asked a question. I guess this is what Mum meant when she said I don't pay enough attention but you know it only happens when I'm not interested. If I like a subject I go mad and read everything about it. I just want to be allowed to study the things I find interesting. D'ya know what I mean?"

"Yeah I do," Melissa responded. "I'm having the same trouble with History at the moment. I loved it when we covered the Tudors but I just can't hack the period we're doing at the moment. It's like I read a whole page of a book and haven't taken in one word. It drives me nuts because then I have to start all over again. Urghhhh!"

The two girls chatted as they walked and it wasn't long before they arrived outside the hospital. Gemma stopped and looked up at the grey, imposing building.

"Whoa. This is it huh? We're really going to do this aren't we?"

"You having doubts Gemma?" Melissa looked at her friend with concern. "Remember we're only asking a question about groups. We're not committing ourselves to anything yet. Is that so bad?"

"I guess not. It's just that I feel so ashamed Mel. I don't want to have to talk about the disgusting things I do. What if people think I'm vile? I'm not sure if I could cope with that."

"Oh Gemma I know it's hard but…" Melissa knew what she wanted to say but she'd never really tried to help anyone like this before. She paused while she gathered her thoughts.

"…but do you think I'm disgusting 'cause I stuff my face? Or that Katee's disgusting because she starves herself until she's just skin and bone? You're being too hard on yourself. I reckon there'll be lots of people at the group who do the same things that we do."

Melissa paused to allow her words to sink in.

"We really don't have to go if you don't want to Gemma but…bulimia's dangerous and well…maybe if you can't go to this group, you should see a doctor instead. I don't want anything to happen to you and I know you need help just like I do."

Melissa came to the end of her sentence and felt nervous. It wasn't comfortable being this honest with Gemma. She was used to telling people what they wanted to hear. She was taking a huge risk by sharing her inner thoughts but she knew she had to do this. She couldn't just sit back and watch her friend harm herself. She was starting to realise that eating disorders were very dangerous illnesses.

"Yeah, you're right Mel," Gemma slowly admitted. "I can't go on living with this…this bulimia. I just hate it so much. Okay, let's do it. Let's go and ask."

The two girls walked through the main hospital doors and up to the front reception desk. Melissa realised she needed to take charge and cleared her throat in preparation. A young woman was sitting behind the desk, her head bowed as she worked but Melissa's light cough caused her to look up. She had a friendly smile on her face and Melissa found herself smiling back.

"Hello…erm…my name is Melissa and I was…um…wondering if your hospital…well not your hospital but this hospital…has any support groups for people with…erm…eating disorders?"

Melissa felt her face heat up as she reached the end of the sentence. The young woman behind the desk was so slim and pretty. She must think that Melissa was a huge, greedy lump of a girl who was in desperate need of help with her eating. It was strange though. The woman didn't look disgusted by Melissa and her smile was warm as she replied to the question.

"Yes, I'm pretty sure we have a support group here Melissa but I don't know the full details. If you go to the third floor, you'll see directions to the Eating Disorders ward, where a nurse should be able to give you a bit more information. She'll be able to tell you when and where the group meets."

The woman paused briefly before continuing.

"Is that okay? Do you want any other help or information?"

"No that's great thank you," Melissa said with relief. "Except…um…do you know if just anyone can join the group?"

"I think they can yes but the nurse would be able to confirm that for you."

The young woman smiled a goodbye at Melissa and then turned to help the nurse who was waiting behind the girls.

"Well that wasn't too bad was it Gemma?" Melissa said, encouragingly. "Let's go get the lift and see what the nurse says. Looks like we're in luck."

Gemma wasn't quite so sure if it was lucky that there was a group but she followed Melissa as she walked from the lobby into the foyer, where the lifts were situated. When a lift finally arrived, they shared it with three doctors and two nurses. Melissa looked at the medical professionals and realised that she didn't feel as scared as she had the day before. The trembling hadn't begun as she'd walked through the hospital doors and her heart seemed to be beating normally. Maybe she felt less afraid because she had Gemma with her? She knew that she had to be strong for her friend. It was as if her own fears and worries had faded so that she could support Gemma. She felt a warm glow inside and a small prickle of pride when she realised that she was using her strength to look after Gemma.

The lift let out a small ping to indicate they had reached the third floor and Gemma and Melissa followed one of the doctors down a long corridor. On the wall opposite, there were a series of plaques indicating different wards. Following the sign to the Eating Disorders ward, the girls found themselves walking along bright, white corridors that seemed endless.

"How on earth do you find your way around a place like this when you first become a nurse?" Gemma asked in amazement.

"I guess it's a bit like school," Melissa replied. "It seemed so huge at first and I was always getting lost but it's easy now."

Gemma giggled.

"It might be easy for you but I'm still arriving everywhere late. I turned up for games ten minutes after the class had started yesterday. Miss Bradon was not amused. I don't think it'd be a good idea for me to become a nurse. People might drop dead while I was trying to find the way to their ward."

At that moment, Melissa decided it was a perfect time to tell Gemma about her childhood dream to become a nurse.

"Gemma, there's something I…er…"

"Omigod we're here. Melissa look at that poor girl," she said, pointing at a young woman walking slowly down the ward. "Oh no. This is awful. She just looks so ill."

Melissa lost her train of thought and immediately tried to hush her friend.

"Gemma, you mustn't stare or point. You'll upset someone," she whispered urgently.

"Was I staring? Oh…I'm sorry. It's just so shocking. I guess I hadn't realised there'd be patients up here. Am I stupid or what?"

"No, not at all. Look…there's a nurse. Let me go and ask about the group."

Melissa again took charge and walked quickly over to the nurse, who seemed to be preparing a strawberry milkshake. This time she asked her question with a little more confidence. The nurse gently placed the glass by the sink and while she was stirring the drink, turned towards Melissa.

"Hello Melissa. My name's Liz. Yes we do have a support group here for people with all different kinds of eating disorders. It's run by our head therapist, Sally Wilkins. She's lovely. The members of the group find her very understanding. Are you interested in joining?"

"Well…er…yes I was and so was…erm…my friend Gemma here."

Liz turned and smiled at Gemma.

"Hello Gemma. Sorry I didn't see you there. I was concentrating on this drink. You have to be so careful with them. If you stop stirring, they can end up a bit lumpy and the girls hate that. It's very important that I don't give them a reason not to drink it, which means I get the wonderful job of stirring each one for at least five minutes."

Gemma smiled. The nurse seemed really friendly. She wasn't sure what she'd expected but it was more along the lines of a strict, angry middle-aged woman who snapped at her patients.

"Why do they have drinks?" she asked. "Don't they eat food at all?"

"Each patient's different Gemma. Some of them aren't yet ready to try solid food and the drinks allow them to receive the nutrition their bodies desperately need. Most of the patients here are having some drinks. As they gradually recover and eat more normally though, we cut them out."

"Does that take long?" Gemma found herself becoming increasingly inquisitive.

"That also depends on the patient Gemma. Some find it harder than others to make progress and need to stay with us a little longer. But it's not just about reaching a healthy weight you know? Each patient needs to have therapy as well, so they can learn why their eating disorder started. It's also important to remember that recovering from an eating disorder isn't a race and often when a patient makes slow progress, it's permanent progress."

Gemma nodded thoughtfully.

"I sort of knew that it wasn't really an illness about food or weight because I've been reading this book on eating disorders. We think that a friend of ours may have anorexia and that was why I was asking so many questions. Sorry about that."

"No need to apologise Gemma. Let me just give this drink to Hannah and then I'll come and find you a leaflet about the group."

The girls watched Liz walk away and then looked around the room. They were in a small kitchen. In the corner was a huge fridge and in the centre of the room there was a table surrounded by six chairs. Melissa started quietly commenting.

"She seems really nice doesn't she? I wonder if she goes to any of the groups?"

"Hmmm…yeah," Gemma answered distractedly. "You know Mel, I think that nurse thinks we're just here about Katee. We're gonna have to explain that we have problems too. I may have led her off track by asking all those questions. I'm really sorry."

"Hey there's no need to feel bad Gemma. What she was saying was really interesting and it might actually help us with Katee. Look…let's just tell her that we need to join the group too. She'll understand."

Melissa had only just finished speaking when Liz entered the room again.

"Here you are girls," she said, holding out two pale green leaflets. "The support group meets every Saturday evening at seven and it's open to anyone who wants to join. You don't even have to have an eating disorder either. We've got quite a few boyfriends and mothers who also come along to learn more. Anyway, these will explain it all in more detail."

As Liz handed over the leaflets, Gemma began to stutter.

"I…er…think I may have misled you a bit. We do have a friend, Katee, who we think has a problem with food but I… um…I also…and so does…er…Melissa here. We have…problems with food. I have… erm…" Gemma's voice grew very quiet. "…I sometimes binge and make myself sick."

"…and I'm just greedy," Melissa interrupted loudly, finishing Gemma's sentence. "I eat too much and I've become disgustingly fat. I look like a blimp."

Gemma looked angrily at her friend.

"You're not disgusting Melissa. Don't say that about yourself. And anyway, nothing's quite as disgusting as making yourself sick after pigging out."

Liz looked at the two girls and smiled reassuringly.

"Neither one of you is disgusting. You both just have some problems with food that you've bravely decided to tackle. You deserve praise, not criticism. Out there is a ward full of girls who use starving, bingeing and vomiting or other methods of self-harm to help them deal with their problems. None of them are 'disgusting'. They're all just suffering from serious illnesses and we're trying to help them learn how to live without them. That's what the support group's about too. Basically, people are able to talk about their issues with food and others can offer support or ideas that might help. Or sometimes they just share their own experiences in return. It's very informal and everyone's really friendly. I think you'll like it if you choose to join us."

"Do you go along Liz?" Gemma asked.

"Oh yes, I go to every session too. Some of the people on the ward join the group and I take them along but there's also another reason why I go." Liz pulled out a chair and sat down at the table. "I had an eating disorder myself for a number of years. I managed to keep it hidden from most of my family and I never had to go into hospital but I had a very rough time when I was at college. I'm actually grateful that I went through it though because it led me into nursing. Now I'm able to share my experiences and use the knowledge I learned about recovery to help a lot of the patients here."

"Whoa!" Gemma and Melissa both stared at the nurse. Their faces showed respect and admiration.

"What kind of eating problems did you have?…If you don't mind me asking," Melissa added quickly.

"Of course I don't mind Melissa," Liz replied. "I'm not ashamed that I had an eating disorder and I'm very happy to talk about it with you. I was like Gemma here. I used to binge on comfort food and then make myself vomit because I felt so guilty for eating."

"Yeah. That's how I feel," Gemma cut in. "I feel so guilty and I have to vomit. I just don't have a choice. I don't want to. It's just that…" Gemma ground to a halt. "Oh I'm sorry. I interrupted you."

"That's okay Gemma. You'll find that people often get excited and speak at the group before another person's finished. For me, the bingeing and vomiting was very occasional at first but it soon increased and I found myself using it as a coping device. You see I was having a difficult time both at home and college, and I started to use the bulimia to block out my feelings. It didn't work though because I still had to cope with a controlling father, all of my degree work and the illness as well."

"Why were you doing a degree if you wanted to be a nurse Liz?" Melissa asked.

"Well, like I said, my Dad was very controlling and he'd decided that I needed to get a degree if I was to have a future. He didn't listen to me when I said that I needed a year out to discover what I really wanted to do."

"So what happened? What made you want to change?" Gemma asked, desperate to know how Liz had recovered.

"My roommate came home one day and found me collapsed on the bathroom floor. I'd passed out after a particularly bad vomiting session. My Dad had phoned me earlier in the day and had shouted at me again for failing my mid-term exams. I just couldn't cope with the pressure and started a massive binge and vomit session that lasted for over three hours. Eventually my body couldn't cope and I collapsed, which was when Jenny found me. She was an amazing friend and I still speak with her every day. We talked for hours and I told her everything. She helped me to find a counsellor and, with therapy, I started to gradually put my life back together again."

"And that's when you found out you wanted to be a nurse and work with eating disorder patients?" Gemma asked.

Liz nodded.

"Wow, that's quite a story. Do you ever feel you want to binge now?"

"For a few years, I used to get a lot of urges and occasionally I did give in to them but my therapist explained to me that everyone has setbacks. They're a natural part of recovery and it's very important that you're gentle on yourself when they happen. It's all about learning that you don't have to be perfect. It's okay to make mistakes. Forgive yourself and then get back on track again."

Liz smiled at them both.

"Does that help a little?"

Gemma and Melissa nodded. Neither of them could quite believe that the nurse sitting in front of them had once had a serious eating disorder. She looked so relaxed and her face glowed with health.

"Would you like to have a quick look around the ward before you leave?" Liz asked. "You could say hello to some of the patients although you may find that a few of them are a bit shy."

Liz saw the hesitation in the girl's faces.

"You don't have to but it might help if you're going to join the group on Saturday."

"I'm just worried that I'll stare," Gemma admitted shyly. "Some of them look so frail and I don't want to embarrass them. This probably sounds stupid but I don't really know what to say to them."

"I can understand that Gemma," Liz said, trying to console her. "But remember it's just the illness that's caused them to lose so much weight. Inside all of these patients is a frightened, confused person who feels very alone. Try to just be yourself and go gently with them. You'll be fine."

Gemma and Melissa looked at each other.

"Shall we?" Melissa asked.

Taking a deep breath, Gemma looked determined.

"Yep, let's go and say hi."

Liz led the two girls out of the kitchen and onto the ward. It contained about ten beds and six of these were occupied. The others were empty but cards and flowers indicated that the patients were just absent from the ward for a while. Liz slowly walked them around the ward and quietly introduced them to each patient. After ten minutes, they had met all but one girl who was sitting alone staring sadly at the strawberry milkshake Liz had just prepared.

"Having problems with it Hannah?" Liz called out.

"I just DON'T want it Liz. My stomach's full and I'm getting so fat. It's not fair. Why won't everyone just leave me alone? I'm so gross already. I don't need this drink. I shouldn't even be here. I'm taking up space that other patients should have. Can't I go home?"

Liz turned to Gemma and Melissa.

"I'm going to have to go and help Hannah with her drink or else she'll still be playing with it by dinner time. It's been lovely meeting you both and I do hope we all get to see you on Saturday. Drop in at any time if you just want to have a chat with any of the girls. We keep them very busy but it can get a little dull for them at times and it's nice to see a new face. Do you know the way out okay?"

Gemma and Melissa nodded together and thanked Liz for all her help. They left the ward and started to walk back to the lift. Gemma looked almost angry.

"Are you okay Gemma?" Melissa enquired. "You look a bit upset. Are you cross that we came?"

"No Mel, I'm very glad that we came but yes I am angry. It's just so horrible that an illness can be so cruel. Does that make sense?"

"I think so…" Melissa replied uncertainly.

"It was when we were meeting everyone," Gemma continued. "And…you know…I was scared to meet them but then when I did, they were just like you and me. I don't know what I expected really. I guess I didn't expect regular people that were just very thin. I hate these illnesses. That girl Hannah was so thin and yet she was convinced that she was fat. I mean she was so thin Mel. She didn't even look like she had enough strength to stand up."

"I know. It's upsetting isn't it? I can understand why you're angry. I found it really hard to look at those girls and think that Katee might end up like that."

"Yeah, that went through my mind too. I am going to help her you know Mel. We can both help if we try. I know it'll be hard but there must be something we can do. Maybe the support group will be able to show us ways to help her too."

"So does that mean you're going to go Gemma?" Melissa said, holding her breath in anticipation.

"Yeah. I guess it does. Are you Mel?"

"Yep. Definitely."

Suddenly a frown creased Gemma's forehead.

"Omigod but what about my date with Tim?"

"Oh no." Melissa looked disappointed. "I'd forgotten about that. Can you go out with him after the support group?" she suggested hopefully.

"No, we'd have missed the beginning of the film. There must be something I can do. I wonder if I could just switch the day? Oh but then he might ask me why and I'd have to make up an excuse. I don't like the idea of lying to him Mel."

Gemma rolled her eyes in annoyance.

"Why does this kind of thing always happen to me? It's like I get a chance to be happy and then something immediately comes along to spoil it."

"Maybe we can find another support group Gemma?" offered Melissa.

"Yeah but I liked Liz and we've already met some of the patients who'll be there. Let me think. There must be a solution."

"I guess you could maybe tell him that you needed to go to the support group to learn about stuff for Katee?" Melissa suggested.

"Hey that's not a bad idea Mel…but I think I'd feel too guilty. I think I'm just going to have to tell him everything. It's a really frightening thought but if he does like me then hopefully he'll understand. If he doesn't want to stick around once he knows my problem then I guess I'll just have to cope. I suppose I wouldn't really want a boyfriend who didn't know the real me."

Melissa beamed at her friend and felt the small prickle of pride return, this time for Gemma. It had been quite some day and she felt that they'd both grown up a little.

21
Meeting Tim

Gemma left Melissa at the bus stop and continued her walk home. They'd spent half an hour visiting Melissa's Dad before leaving the hospital and now her mind was alive with a hundred different thoughts. The trip to the Eating Disorders ward had opened her eyes to the reality of anorexia and she'd been horrified by her reaction. The terrifying thinness of all the patients had scared her and at first she'd wanted to run away. Would Katee end up that ill?

Her mind was also filled with thoughts of Tim. She'd only met him once but already he felt important to her and talking about her eating problems was going to be very difficult. Gemma knew she had to tell him soon or else she'd lose her courage and start lying. Stopping by a low wall, she started to search through her bag for any spare money. At the bottom, squeezed into a crease, Gemma discovered a pound coin. The decision had been made for her. She now had enough money to call Tim and ask him to meet her. Her stomach did a somersault. Before she could change her mind, she started to look around for a phone box. She'd only walked for a couple of minutes when she spotted one on the other side of the road. Screwing up all her courage, Gemma crossed the road and opened the door. She took a minute to arrange herself so that she was comfortable and let her breathing calm down a little. Her heart was pounding and small beads of sweat were forming on her forehead.

She felt annoyed with herself.

Get a grip on yourself Gemma. What are you so uptight about? It's only Tim. Calm down and just make the call.

Picking up the phone, Gemma started to dial the number she had now committed to memory. Tim answered on the third ring.

"Tim! Hi! It's me…Gemma."

"Gemma hi. You okay?"

"Well kind of but…erm…Tim there's something I really need to tell you and I just have to do it today. Could we meet? Maybe in the coffee shop again?"

"Sure that's fine. Do you want to meet now? You seem worried. Has something happened?" Tim sounded concerned.

"Now would be good Tim. Can you get out of work?"

"Yeah that's no problem. We're open late tonight and I was just going to take my break anyway. Shall I meet you in…what? Say five minutes maybe?"

"Give me ten because I'm in Ambridge Drive and it'll take me a while to get to the library."

"Okay. I'll see you then."

Tim hung up the phone and immediately felt worried. Gemma had sounded distant. Maybe she'd changed her mind about the date. After all, it had been arranged very quickly. He'd tormented himself the night before, trying to work out if he should ask her out. Maybe she wasn't ready yet or maybe she just didn't like him enough. He grabbed his coat from the cupboard and went to inform the Head Librarian that he would be out for an hour.

According to Tim's watch, Gemma arrived at the coffee shop exactly eight minutes after he had sat down in a booth with his coffee. He'd waited outside for a while but had felt too self-conscious and thought it might be better if he saved a quiet table in the corner. Gemma slipped into the seat opposite, where a cup of coffee was waiting for her.

"Thanks for meeting me here Tim. I really do have something important to tell you. Although it's not going to be easy for me to say this."

"Why don't I say it for you Gemma?" Tim jumped in. "You just don't want to go out with me right? It's okay…I think I probably asked you too soon. I'm very happy to wait if you're not ready. I…well I really like you and I'd be very happy to…just be friends if that's what you want."

Gemma smiled at the young man sitting opposite her. She could see that he was feeling nervous and anxious. His napkin was in shreds by his coffee cup and he was picking at the pieces of skin by his thumbnails.

"No Tim. That's not it at all. I was really excited when you asked me out but then something else happened today and I knew I had to talk to you. It may be that when you've heard what I have to say, you won't actually want to go out with me. In fact you might not want anything more to do with me ever again."

Tim looked puzzled. "Well I can't think of anything so dramatic that would make me change my mind. Have you murdered someone?" he joked.

Despite her nervousness, Gemma smiled.

"I don't think it's quite that bad but it is something that I feel very ashamed about."

"Okay. Well why don't you just go ahead and tell me? It's always better to get things out into the open. Take your time and then just blurt it all out."

Gemma took another deep breath. Her life seemed to be nothing but confrontations at the moment. It would almost be funny if it wasn't so nerve-wracking.

"Whoa. This is hard. Okay, let me start. You know that Katee has an eating disorder that we think is anorexia? Well I was reading that book and…." Gemma paused to try to control the shaking that had started. "…and I think that it looks like I have a problem myself."

Gemma paused again as she heard a sharp intake of breath from Tim. She looked at him and waited to see if he would speak.

"Carry on Gemma. I'm listening."

"Well I was reading this chapter on bulimia and I recognised the symptoms in myself. Tim…occasionally I…I binge and then make myself sick. I know that's really disgusting but I do it because I can't deal with the way my Mum treats me and it's sort of an escape. I'm not making excuses though 'cause I know it's disgusting. I'm going to get help though," she continued, trying to sound positive. "I went to the hospital today with Melissa to see if they have a support group and they do. We've both decided to join because Melissa has problems with overeating and I…well I have bulimia and we both want to learn about ways to help Katee and…and…"

Gemma drew to a halt. She'd said enough. If Tim wanted to walk out now he could. After a moment's silence, he spoke.

"Well I certainly wasn't expecting you to tell me that Gemma. You know it was really brave of you to go to the hospital today and even braver to tell me about it. I guess I'm shocked because you just seem really healthy and so pretty and slim and I assumed that it was…you know…obvious when a person has an eating disorder. Sorry. That sounds really stupid. As if I expect people to wear signs around their necks saying 'Hey Everyone! I'm A Bulimic!'"

Tim thought for a few seconds and then suddenly burst into speech again.

"I'm so sorry Gemma. That was a really insensitive thing to say. I didn't mean to offend you. Have I offended you? I guess I don't really know the etiquette about eating disorders. Is it okay to call someone with bulimia 'a bulimic' or is that really offensive?"

"No Tim, you didn't offend me. I don't really know myself yet. I guess I'm still learning to accept that I have bulimia and haven't even thought of myself as a bulimic. It does sound kind of horrible but I guess it's just a word and I have to accept it until I'm better. I'm going to have to be careful at the group though. I don't want to say anything that'll upset anyone."

"Oh I'm sure you wouldn't do that," Tim added emphatically.

Gemma gave a brief smile, which faded quickly.

"Bulimia can be hidden for years you know Tim but it does some terrible things to your body. All your teeth can rot and you can have a heart attack or kidney failure. It's just so frightening. That's why I knew I had to tell Melissa. And when I'd told her then she said we had to find out about help and then when we went to the hospital they told us the support group was on Saturday and that's the day of our date."

Gemma finished her sentence and realised she'd run out of breath.

"Would you have told me about the bulimia and the support group if it hadn't been on Saturday Gemma?" Tim asked.

Gemma felt uncomfortable. She wasn't actually sure about how to answer that question. She probably would have tried to keep the truth from Tim for a while longer and maybe that would have been wrong.

"I don't know Tim. I guess I just felt so ashamed of my behaviour I didn't want to have to admit to it."

"We all do things at times we're not particularly proud of but it's usually for a reason. I mean, you could have turned to drugs or smoking to try and block out your feelings but I guess your 'solution' was the bulimia."

"Not a great choice huh?"

"That's not what's important Gemma. It's the fact that you've had the courage to come forward and ask for help that matters. And I do feel really pleased…well…honoured I guess that you felt able to trust me with all this."

"Do you know that's what the nurse at the hospital said? That it's really brave to ask for help. At the time I thought that was so weird but now I'm beginning to understand what she meant."

"If you ever want me to come along to a support group, just as a friend, then…you know…I'd be very happy to do that," Tim offered quietly.

Gemma was touched. She had been very unsure about his reaction but so far he seemed to understand. Was he just being kind? She guessed that only time would tell. He did seem very genuine though. She giggled inwardly. She felt so old and experienced, trying to work out if the man sitting opposite her was genuine.

"Thanks Tim. I'm going with Melissa this week but maybe in the future it'd be okay if you came too?"

Tim smiled. "It must've been really tough telling me all that. I feel like I ought to make some kind of confession to make it even…um…I did smoke once but the taste made me feel sick so I gave it up…um… I guess I'm just really boring really. I suppose I am having a few problems with my Dad who just wants me to get on with doing a Law degree and stop faffing about at the library but I know what I want to do and it's definitely not Law."

"Your Dad sounds a bit like my Mum. She's convinced that she knows what's best for me. It's really hard to get my opinion heard at home. Does that make me sound like a selfish brat?"

"No way Gemma. You're not selfish. In fact, I think you're really understanding. Go on. Tell me some more about your Mum."

They sat in the coffee shop for half an hour while Gemma tried to explain about her home life. Eventually, Tim looked at his watch and saw that he needed to get back to the library.

"I'm sorry Gemma. I really hate to say this but I've got to go back to work. Did you want to re-arrange our date or just leave it for a while? Either way is okay with me."

"I'd like to set another day if that's alright with you Tim," Gemma replied nervously.

"That'd be great. How about Friday night?" Tim said with enthusiasm.

"I'll have to check with my Mum. Sometimes she wants me home on Fridays because my Gran visits. Can I give you a call?"

"Sure. I'm really sorry that I've got to run. It's just my boss you know? Call me any time Gemma. It's always good to chat with you."

Tim stood up from the table and paused awkwardly. Gemma looked up at him, slightly puzzled. Just as she was about to ask if there was a problem, Tim leaned over and lightly kissed her on the cheek before dashing for the door. Gemma felt shocked and confused. Had Tim just kissed her? Was it a proper kiss? It felt like the kind of peck on the cheek that friends gave each other. He was probably just trying to reassure her that it was good she'd shared her feelings and that he was proud of her.

She had wondered if telling him would be wise but now she was pretty certain it had been a good move. It was a relief that she no longer carried the burden of keeping her bulimia a secret. However there was one person she could never tell. Her mother would never understand that bulimia was a real illness. Gemma shuddered inwardly at how angry her Mum would be if she ever found out that her daughter binged and then made herself sick. She looked at her watch and was shocked by the time. As she broke into a run, she realised that she was going to be late for dinner again. She sat down on the bus and finally acknowledged the fact that she was actually very scared of her own mother.

22
Supporting Each Other

Saturday seemed to come around much too fast for Gemma. She'd had a wonderful time with Tim the night before and hadn't wanted the evening to end. He had picked her up at seven and they'd seen a movie at the cinema in town. Afterwards, they'd picked up a portion of chips from the takeaway next door and sat in Tim's car to share them. At first,

Gemma had felt scared. She hadn't eaten any chips since she'd begun her diet in the summer. She watched Tim tuck hungrily into the salty, glistening chips and she started to feel rumbles of hunger herself. As she watched him eat, she realised that she desperately wanted to try one too. She chose one of the smallest that she could see and then carefully tasted the steaming hot fried chip.

The taste was incredible and Gemma felt an urge to cram the entire portion into her mouth at once. She was glad that Tim was with her because she knew that if she'd been alone, she could have started to binge. Slowly, she allowed herself to share the chips with Tim. As she ate, the need to binge started to fade and she felt tremendous relief. Maybe she should talk about this experience at the support group. She wasn't quite sure why the urge to binge had started or why it had faded but she felt as though she'd fought a small battle and won.

Tim and Gemma chatted for an hour until finally, at 10.30, she realised that if they didn't make a move she'd miss her curfew. Her Mum hadn't been too pleased when she'd asked if she could go on a date but when Tim arrived, her mood had changed. She'd been very impressed by the well-spoken, neatly dressed young man who stood at the door asking if Gemma was ready. However, Gemma knew her Mum and felt sure she would soon lose patience if she was late.

Gemma didn't get much sleep that night as her head was buzzing with thoughts. Tim was the first boy she'd been out with and it was very exciting to spend time with him. As the dawn of Saturday started to break, her thoughts changed though. Her mind began to focus on the support group instead and she felt increasingly worried. She'd told her Mum that she was going to Melissa's house for the evening. She hated lying but she knew there was no way she could tell her mother the truth. She hadn't told anyone yet about her realisation on the bus. She really didn't want to face the possibility that she was scared of her own Mum but deep down, she knew it was true. She was even starting to wonder if she actually loved her. Maybe the group would be able to help her come to terms with some of these new feelings she was having.

∞∞∞∞

Gemma met Melissa outside the hospital ten minutes before seven that evening and they chatted nervously as they made their way up to the second floor. The leaflet had said that the group met in a room near the Coronary Care Ward. It only took them a few minutes to find a conference style room that contained a large circle of wooden chairs. They were the first to arrive and sat quietly while they waited for the other members.

During the next ten minutes, Gemma and Melissa watched twelve people slowly drift in and greet one another. They all smiled shyly at the two newcomers and a few even introduced themselves. Gemma noticed that the majority of the group members were a normal weight. In fact it was only the three girls who arrived with Liz that were actually underweight.

For five minutes, everyone chatted as they found chairs and waited for the therapist to appear. Shortly after seven, a smartly dressed middle-aged woman scurried into the room and closed the door behind her.

"Sorry I'm late everyone. I had car trouble again. I'm just going to have to ask for a pay increase so that I can get that heap of junk fixed."

She looked around the room.

"Well it looks as though we have a couple of newcomers so I think I should introduce myself first. My name is Sally Wilkins and I'm a therapist who specialises in the treatment of eating disorders. This is our group and we meet once a week to discuss our problems with various eating disorders. Can I ask everyone else to introduce themselves now and say just a line or two about why they're with us? Sandra, would you like to start?"

An attractive young woman in her early 20's smiled at Sally.

"Okay. I guess I could go first. Well my name is Sandra and I've been coming to the group now for over five months. I have bulimia and I also self-harm at times."

She turned to the woman on her left.

"Debbie? Your go."

Gemma recognised one of the girls from the Eating Disorders ward.

"My name's Debbie and I'm anorexic. I've been coming to the group for about four weeks and have been an in-patient at the hospital for two months. I feel really fat and I hate my doctor."

Sally looked concerned.

"Thanks Debbie for that introduction. I'm sorry that you're upset with your doctor. Can you tell us more about that in a minute when we all discuss how our week has been?"

The young girl nodded miserably and Sally asked the next person along to continue. He was one of only two men at the group.

"Hi. My name is Jeff and I'm a compulsive eater. I've been coming to the group for nearly a year now and it's really helped me to get my eating under control. Jan? You're next."

Gemma was surprised by the age of the next member of the group. She'd believed that eating disorders were only a teenagers problem but Jan was a woman in her late fifties.

"Hello. My name is Janice although everybody calls me Jan. I've been coming to the group for a couple of months. My doctor advised me to join. I've had problems for ten years and finally decided to get help last year. Bulimia has caused me so many problems and I'm having a lot of dental treatment at the moment. I want to beat this illness and that's why I'm here."

"Thanks Jan. Lisa?" Sally continued to encourage the group to speak.

"Hi, my name's Lisa and I'm anorexic. Kim?"

The group carried on introducing themselves until everyone had spoken. Sally then turned to Gemma and Melissa and smiled.

"Would you like to introduce yourselves to the group?"

Gemma and Melissa looked at one another, each one hoping the other would speak first. After a brief pause, Melissa decided to be brave. She wanted to help Gemma and felt that if she took the lead then her friend would follow. She started to speak before she could change her mind.

"My name is Melissa and I'd like to join the group because I have a problem with over-eating. I just can't seem to stop eating even though I want to lose weight."

Gemma felt very proud of her friend's courage and quickly gave her own short introduction.

"Hi everyone. I'm Gemma and I think I may have bulimia. I occasionally binge and then make myself sick. I hate doing this and I want to learn how to stop it from ever happening again."

Sally waited a moment in case the two newcomers wanted to say anything more.

"Thank you both for introducing yourselves and on behalf of us all, I'd like to welcome you to our group. It's very informal here and everyone's free to share any worries they have or talk about the progress they're making in recovery. The meeting usually lasts about an hour and then you can stay for coffee afterwards if you want to meet some of the other members."

Sally paused for a minute.

"Okay well that's the introductions done so why don't we start talking about our week and how it went? Debbie, would you like to start? You said you had a problem with your doctor?"

"Yeah. I really don't think anyone's listening to me at all. I just can't cope with the piles of food they're giving me. I'm putting on tonnes of weight and I want it to stop. I'm so fat and I just want to be left alone."

Debbie ground to a halt. Her eyes were blazing with anger and Gemma could see that she was trying to fight back tears. She wanted to say something that would help but didn't know where to start. Looking around the group she saw that many of the members had their heads bowed. Others were looking around awkwardly hoping that someone else would speak. Sally left a few moments of silence to see if anyone would speak up and try to help Debbie.

"Does anyone have anything they want to say to Debbie?" Sally finally said, trying to encourage the group to work together. "Can anyone identify with her feelings? Kim? Lisa?"

Lisa looked at Debbie and smiled.

"Yeah, I can really identify with Debbie's feelings. I think they make us put on weight too quickly here and you just don't get enough time to cope with one weight increase before you go up again. I know this probably doesn't make much sense but if they just allowed us to put on weight a bit slower, I don't think it'd be so scary. It's like I need to adjust to my new size before it changes again."

Kim and Debbie nodded fiercely in agreement.

"It's just too much too quickly," Kim agreed. "Is there anything you can do Liz? Maybe speak to the doctors for us?"

Liz looked thoughtful.

"I understand how tough it is but the hospital has a set treatment programme for anorexia. If they slow it down then the time you have to stay here will get longer. They've set the weight increase at a healthy level and although I can have a word with the doctors, I think they'll still want you to aim for the same weight gain each week."

Sally listened to Liz's comments before speaking herself.

"Maybe we need to organise more therapy sessions to deal with the body image problems you're having. Remember you do need to gain this weight because your bodies are severely undernourished. The more important point here is actually the way you feel about your weight gain. Would you like me to arrange some more therapy sessions on the ward?"

The three girls looked at each other and shrugged. Debbie spoke first.

"I guess that might help but there's part of me that doesn't even want to do the therapy in case I get more used to being bigger. I hate being fat and I don't know that I want anyone to try to convince me that it's right to be this size."

"No one can force you to believe anything Debbie. We're just trying to show you that the anorexia is lying to you. It wants to convince you that a normal healthy weight is wrong. It wants you to believe that you're bad if you eat. These are lies and there are ways that you can shout back at the anorexia when it says these cruel things to you."

Debbie shrugged dismissively again and Gemma could see that she was unconvinced. Maybe this was how Katee felt? Maybe she thought that everyone was just trying to turn her into someone she didn't want to be. She could see Katee's defensiveness and anger in Debbie. Thinking about it though, wouldn't she feel angry if she thought everyone was pressuring her all the time?

Gemma heard Sally speak again.

"Okay Debbie we'll see about increasing the body image sessions and remember you can talk with your key worker at any time about your feelings. Don't try and cope with them alone when you can have some extra help."

Sally paused to let her words sink in and then looked around the group again.

"Does anyone else want to talk about their week? Jan?"

Jan nodded. "It's not been a good week for me at all. I had some bad days at the dentist on Monday and Tuesday but it was my therapist appointment that was really painful."

Sally spoke very gently. "Do you want to share that with us Jan?"

"Okay but I might get a bit emotional. The session was difficult because we're currently looking at why my bulimia started and I'm remembering some…things from my childhood. They're really painful and I don't know that I can cope. My…father treated me badly and it looks like I used the bulimia to deal with that. What I don't understand though is what happened after my therapy session."

"And what was that Jan?" Jeff asked compassionately.

Gemma was impressed by the gentle way everyone worked together. They were carefully trying to encourage each other to speak out about their problems.

"Well I spent four hours bingeing and purging. It was like I couldn't stop. I knew that I was doing my teeth even more damage and was eating a whole week's food but I couldn't stop. I felt disgusted with myself for talking about my Dad and what he did. I felt ashamed and like I was betraying him and I just wished I hadn't said anything."

"People often feel like that when they start to talk about painful experiences from the past Jan," Sally said. "It can feel like you're reliving the events all over again. You mustn't let that put you off talking though."

"May I speak Sally?" Jeff asked shyly.

"Sure Jeff. Please go ahead."

"Thanks. Okay Jan, well I went through this too when I was talking about some of the bullying I had at school. People used to pick on me because I was large and that really depressed me, which then meant I ate even more."

Gemma heard Melissa's sharp intake of breath. She had obviously identified with Jeff's story.

"I really didn't want to tell my therapist about some of the cruel things that had been said and done to me as a child," Jeff continued. "But she explained that bad memories are like splinters. They need to come to the surface. If they stay buried, they just continue to hurt you every day. When you talk about bad memories though, it's like you're slowly removing these splinters and that means you can start to heal again."

"Thanks Jeff," Sally said. "That's a really good analogy."

"But why did I binge and purge so badly if I was supposed to feel better?" Jan asked, still confused.

"You don't feel better instantly Jan," Sally replied. "It takes time. Right now your splinters or memories are coming to the surface and they're very painful. You're looking at them for the first time in years. It's going to hurt because facing your past is tough. Your way of coping with tough situations is to binge and purge but remember that you now know people who care and want to help."

"I know what you're going through," Sandra spoke for the first time. "I was abused by my Uncle and I tried to deal with it by turning to bulimia. When I binged, I was trying to bury my feelings and when I threw up, I was trying to get rid of them in a different way. I wanted to be 'clean' and needed to get everything out of me, including the feelings. When I was sick it was like I was getting rid of my Uncle too. Does that make any sense?"

The whole conversation was making sense to Gemma and she was beginning to feel less alone. She could relate to these people and didn't feel so ashamed any more. She was amazed at how honest and open they could be and she wanted to join in. She needed to share something herself. Very nervously, she started to speak.

"I know I'm new here so I don't know everyone's story but I just wanted to say that I'm really glad I came. I've been…doing what Sandra's saying.

I block out my feelings by bingeing and then throwing up. I'm having some problems with my Mum and just can't cope with the way I feel. Um…that's all I wanted to say. Thanks," Gemma finished in a rush.

She looked up to see Sally smiling and thanking her for contributing to the group. For the next half hour, various members continued to share their experiences. Melissa even shared some of her feelings when Jeff talked about what it was like to be overweight.

All too quickly the hour had passed and Sally was asking Liz to close the meeting. The group ended with a final chance for everyone to speak. They were encouraged to name one task they wanted to achieve the following week.

Debbie wanted to get through a weighing session without crying.

Sandra wanted to manage a binge free day.

Jeff was going to try to ride on a bus. Melissa was horrified to hear that cruel comments had left him feeling afraid to even travel on public transport.

As they went around the group, Gemma started to feel nervous. What could she try as her task for the week? They had already reached Melissa.

"I'm going to try and have a chocolate free day on Wednesday," Melissa announced.

Suddenly, Gemma knew what she wanted to try.

"I want to try and eat one of the foods that I've been avoiding since I started dieting. I had chips yesterday and now I want to try a piece of cake again."

"That sounds very sensible Gemma," Liz said. "If you're hungry and craving certain foods then you're more likely to binge. If you're going to stop the bingeing and vomiting then you need to tackle it from all angles, and that'll mean eating a healthy nutritious diet too."

Gemma smiled. She really was glad they'd joined this group. She and Melissa even stayed for twenty minutes after the meeting broke up. The three girls went back to their ward with Liz but many of the other members stayed for coffee. Gemma started talking to Sandra and she saw Melissa wander off and begin chatting with Jeff.

After a while, Sally joined them and asked if she could have a word with Gemma and Melissa.

"I just wanted to welcome the two of you to the group again and say that if there's anything you specifically need help with, just get in touch. This is my number at the hospital and we can always arrange a time when you can come in for a chat."

Sally handed them each a card and then, with a final smile, she left. Gemma and Melissa looked at each other and grinned.

"I do feel a bit silly," Gemma said.

"Why's that?" asked Melissa.

"Well I was really freaking out about the group and it's actually very good. Nothing to be scared of at all. Isn't it amazing how you can blow everything so out of proportion? Thanks for pushing me into coming Mel. I know I wasn't very easy at times."

"Well you weren't exactly enthusiastic but what does it matter now? We got here and it was good. I really like that Jeff. He's been through such a lot you know? I thought I got teased but whoa, it's nothing compared to his life. Urghhh. Some people are just so cruel."

The two girls continued to chat as they wandered back to the bus stop.

"D'you want to go and get something to eat?" Gemma asked.

"Hmmmm. Yeah but let's go for something healthier. How about we get jacket potatoes from that new takeaway place on the corner? I could have cottage cheese and sweetcorn."

"What a good idea," Gemma replied with enthusiasm. "I'll go for baked beans."

Melissa smiled.

"We can eat in and then you can tell me about your date with Tim. And I want all the details okay? No skipping over the juicy bits."

Gemma smiled with embarrassment.

"I think we should just discuss the group and our tasks for the week. You don't really want to know that Tim kissed me do you?"

Gemma couldn't help but giggle. She'd finally rendered Melissa speechless.

23
The Voice

Katee's life was settling into a routine. Friday night had been no different to any other evening that week. Her Dad hadn't even looked at her when she had arrived home from school. In fact, he hadn't spoken to her since the day she'd thrown her dinner at the wall. Strangely though, she felt relieved. She couldn't face his rage any more and this coldness was easier to cope with. His angry promise that they'd eat their meals together as a family hadn't come true either. Every evening he'd taken his food into the lounge and watched the television while he ate alone.

Jane had been valiantly trying to encourage her daughter to eat and had made salads and other low calorie meals all week. Katee had felt relieved and would pick at a few lettuce leaves before she tipped the rest into the bin and disappeared upstairs into her room again.

The self-harming had continued all week and so had the exercising. Katee wasn't even sure why she had to hurt herself so much but the urges were overpowering. The 'voice' filled her head with such valid reasons. It told her that she was still fat and needed to exercise. Then it commanded her to cut herself because it told her that she was a bad person. Whatever it said, its words always seemed to ring so true.

"You shouldn't have eaten that apple at lunch or the lettuce leaves this evening. You must punish yourself and you must do it NOW!

You shouldn't have talked with Melissa and Gemma…They hate you! Everyone hates you! Hurt yourself and do it NOW!

Your Dad and Mum are angry with you...You upset everyone... You must punish yourself and you must do it NOW!"

The number of cuts on Katee's arm was growing. When one began to heal, the 'voice' simply told her to cut again. Looking down at the criss-crossed red lines, she felt sick. She couldn't even count the number of marks any longer. She knew that she had completely lost control. The 'voice' had taken over and she was now just its servant.

∞∞∞∞

Katee awoke early on Saturday morning with her stomach rumbling and the new cuts stinging. Recollections of the night before hit her and she felt deeply depressed. Her body was achingly tired but she couldn't let herself rest and instead forced herself out of bed to start exercising.

At nine o'clock, she heard the phone ring in the distance and paused for breath. Her face was flushed and sweat was running down her back. She crept to the door and listened. When she heard her name, it was like a sharp kick to the stomach. Why was her Mum talking about her? What was going on?

She only had to wait five minutes to find out. There was a quiet knock on her door and she heard her mother's voice call out.

"Katee? Are you awake honey?"

Katee opened the door and let her Mum into the room.

"I'm glad you're up love. I need to talk with you."

"Who was that on the phone Mum?"

"That's what I need to talk to you about darling. It was the doctor's surgery. They want to see you this morning because they have your test results back from the hospital. They've booked you in for 10.15 this morning, so if you get ready you've time for some breakfast before we have to go."

Katee started to shake and fire out angry questions.

"Why do they want to see me? What did the hospital say? I don't want to go. There's nothing wrong with me. You can't make me go you know."

"Katee if you don't go to the surgery, Dr. Morgan said he'd come here. We might just as well go to save him the trouble. I'll come with you. It'll be okay."

Katee's anger faded as she realised once again that she was cornered. Fear took over and she began to shake. Like a small child, she started to beg her Mum to help her.

"I don't want to go Mum. Please don't make me. Can't you tell the doctor I'm fine? Please? Please Mum. PLEASE!"

Jane looked at her daughter and it felt as though her heart would break. She knew that Katee needed the doctor's help but she felt like she was betraying her. She knew how scared Katee was but if they didn't take action now then the consequences could be terrifying.

"I'm sorry Katee. I have no choice. I've got to take you to see the doctor but I won't leave you. I promise I'll be there for you every moment."

Katee's mood changed again when she heard that her Mum wouldn't help her. The anger returned and she heard herself spit out cruel and hurtful remarks.

"You hate me don't you? All you want is to get rid of me! Why don't you just leave me alone? You're so horrible! I hate you! I hate you more than anyone in the world!"

Katee couldn't believe what she was saying. It didn't even feel like she was the one talking. Had the 'voice' taken over completely?

Jane was getting quite used to the sudden changes in her daughter's mood. Outbursts like the one she'd just witnessed had been happening all week. She didn't think Katee could control her moods any longer and so was trying very hard not to take the comments personally. She sensed that she needed to remain calm and caring rather than show her daughter anger and frustration.

"I'm sorry love. I'm not trying to hurt you. I'm only doing what the doctor requested. I can't ignore his phone call. He's going to see you today and if we try to avoid him then he'll just drop round here. Please get dressed and we'll go and get this meeting over with. It'll only take a few minutes."

Jane smiled and left the room. Katee grudgingly started to get dressed. Her clothes were becoming baggier by the day. She couldn't wear her favourite jeans any longer because they were just too loose. She tightened the belt on her smallest pair of trousers and pulled on three jumpers. A shiver of fear ran through her as she caught a glimpse of reality.

She'd lost so much weight recently that none of her clothes fitted any longer. How could the 'voice' tell her that she was fat if all her clothes were falling off? Was the doctor going to be angry that she'd lost more weight? Why did he want to see her? What were the results like? What if they were really bad?

A lone tear trickled down Katee's face but she angrily brushed it away. She didn't cry and besides she wasn't really alone was she? She had the 'voice' with her. Why should she care what some doctor said? She had her own inbuilt friend to help her lose weight and get thin.

Her momentary glimpse of reality had passed and she was once again controlled by the 'voice'. She shrugged on another cardigan and went downstairs.

"Katee, do you really need to wear all those jumpers?" her Mum asked. "You'll boil at the doctors. They always have the heat up in there."

"Leave me alone Mum. I'm cold okay?" Katee snapped.

Jane bit back her immediate response. Why was Katee so cold? The day was actually quite mild and they also had the heating on in the house. Perhaps this was something else she should mention to the doctor.

∞∞∞∞

Katee looked around the waiting room. It felt as if she spent half her life in doctor's surgeries now. It was less busy there on Saturday and she was the only patient waiting to see the doctor. It was just a couple of minutes before he appeared at the door and called her through into his room.

While Katee and Jane settled in the chairs opposite his desk, Dr. Morgan flicked through a set of papers.

"Thanks for coming in this morning Katee. I asked to see you because I've received your test results back from the hospital and I'm afraid it's not good news."

The doctor paused to let his words sink in before he continued.

"Your blood tests show that you're severely depleted in all the vital minerals, especially iron, and that you have mild anaemia which needs to be treated. Your ECG results also weren't very good. They showed an irregularity in your heartbeat that we're concerned about."

Again, the doctor paused and looked directly at Katee. She tried to hold his gaze defiantly but just couldn't maintain eye contact for long. What did it matter if her heartbeat was irregular or that she had anaemia? At least she was losing weight. That was all that was important.

However, his next comment shook Katee to the core.

"Katee, I believe that you have anorexia nervosa. The tests have backed up my initial thoughts. Also, Dr. Elliot at the hospital noted signs of anorexia when he carried out the tests and has advised that you spend a few weeks in the Eating Disorders ward. Apparently they have a very good therapist there, Sally Wilkins, who he thinks may be able to help."

Katee tried to speak but she just couldn't form any words. The doctor continued talking.

"Because of your heart irregularities, we need to get you into hospital as soon as possible so that you can be monitored. Your blood tests indicated a very limited diet and we also need to sort that out too. I've arranged for a bed to be available for you tomorrow morning."

Jane was now as stunned as her daughter. Even though she'd felt certain that something was wrong with Katee, to have it officially diagnosed was frightening. The words 'anorexia nervosa' kept repeating over and over in her mind. Katee had a serious illness. It was so serious that they actually wanted to admit her to hospital.

"I've failed my daughter haven't I doctor? Isn't anorexia always the mother's fault?" Jane said shakily. "What did I do wrong?"

"Mrs. Quinn, this really isn't the time to start pointing fingers. Anorexia develops for many different reasons and the hospital therapist will be able to help Katee uncover why she turned to the illness. The fact that

you brought Katee to see me shows that you care and want to help.
I can give you some addresses so that you can discover more about
anorexia and maybe join a group for parents of sufferers."

"Thank you doctor," Jane replied numbly. "But what do we do now? Do
we pack Katee a bag? Will she be in hospital long do you think?"

"The hospital staff are expecting you at ten tomorrow morning. If
Katee's able to co-operate then she really won't have to stay there long.
As soon as her heartbeat is more regular and her mineral levels improve,
she'll be able to continue her treatment at home. At the moment
though her health is deteriorating and she's in danger so we need to
keep her safe."

Katee still hadn't said a word. Dr. Morgan turned to her.

"I know this must come as a shock Katee but I'm afraid it's necessary
right now. Is there anything you want to ask or say?"

"I'm not going into any hospital," Katee said defiantly. "I'm fine and I
don't need to go."

"I'm afraid that you do need to go Katee and if you don't go voluntarily
then we will have to section you."

In a much quieter voice, Katee spoke again.

"What's a section?"

"Sectioning is when we have to take a patient into hospital against their
will. If we know that their health is at risk or that they're a danger to
themselves then we have to take them into hospital. If they won't come
voluntarily, we have to make the decision for them and admit them using a
court order. It's not pleasant so it's much better for you to go voluntarily."

"So I have no choice then? I have to go into hospital whether I want to or not?"

"I'm afraid so Katee but as I say, it won't be for long and they've got a really good Eating Disorders ward there."

Katee didn't hear any of the remaining conversation between her mother and the doctor. She was no longer in the room with them. She was alone with the 'voice' in its world. And it was shouting.

"How could you let this happen? How could you let them take you into hospital? You know what they're going do, don't you? They're going to force you to eat piles of food. You're going to get fatter and fatter until you're this HUGE disgusting fat blob! You're an idiot for letting them win! A stupid idiotic fat girl! You're going to have to really punish yourself tonight and this is what you're going to do..."

24
Admission

Katee had walked out of the doctor's surgery in a daze. She couldn't believe that she was being admitted to hospital. The 'voice' had promised her she'd be fine. That no one would be able to stop her losing weight. It was wrong. She was devastated. Thoughts of running away flitted in and out of her head. Wouldn't it just be easier to disappear than to be admitted? She knew that running away wouldn't solve anything but somehow it made her feel better to think she still had options.

Jane had also been very shocked when she heard that their daughter needed a hospital admission. She knew that Brian would think the doctor was over-reacting again but maybe now they had a diagnosis, he'd take the situation more seriously.

The afternoon had passed for Katee in a haze of packing and tears. Every time she thought about the hospital, she would start to shake and feel misty eyed. She hated herself for crying but just wasn't able to control her emotions. She felt scared, alone and most of all betrayed. The taunting 'voice' had let her down and yet she still found herself listening to its words. Even those were confusing today though.

It praised her for losing more weight and for cutting out so much food. The test results proved just how hard she'd fought to stop eating and whenever the 'voice' praised Katee, she felt a flicker of pride. Losing weight gave her a happy buzz but pleasing the 'voice' was the best feeling of all.

Her inner 'voice' wasn't happy about the hospital admission though and by three o'clock that afternoon, Katee was bleeding from many new cuts. She hadn't even stopped to think that the doctors might notice them. All that mattered was doing exactly what the 'voice' said and that day it wanted her to punish herself.

∞∞∞∞

Sunday morning came around much too quickly for Katee. She'd been awake for most of the night, exercising and cutting but she still felt bad. She'd heard her parents arguing late into the night and then at 2 am, the front door had slammed. She didn't know where her father had gone but he certainly wasn't home when she went downstairs to get some black coffee. It was just her Mum who greeted her.

"Hi sweetheart. Did you sleep okay? Your Dad's not going to be coming to the hospital with us this morning. It'll just be you and me but that's okay isn't it?"

"Yeah that's fine Mum," Katee agreed. "I didn't want him to come anyway. He'd have just shouted at the doctors or been horrible or something."

"Katee, don't speak about your father like that," Jane said instinctively.

Anger started to bubble up in Katee.

"Why not Mum? You know what he's like. He's cruel and vicious and I hate him." Turning on her heels, Katee ran back up to her room.

Jane wanted to deny that her daughter's words were true but could she really do that? Brian's behaviour was going out of control. The previous evening had been a nightmare. She'd tried to calmly explain Katee's problems but he wouldn't even listen. Relentlessly slamming his fist on the table, he'd told her that if she took Katee to the hospital she'd have to go alone. There was nothing wrong with their daughter. She was just a self-centred, lazy girl who wanted time off school. Jane couldn't believe what she was hearing. When had he become so bitter and cruel or had he always been like this? Maybe she'd just lived her whole life in denial.

She was relieved when he later stormed out of the house. She was even tempted to get the locks changed so that he couldn't return but knew she wasn't able to do that. Brian seemed so different now. This wasn't the man she'd fallen in love with and this certainly wasn't the man who'd cherished and loved their young children for so long. Something had happened in the last few years and losing his job had been the final straw. He'd become pushy and difficult and had started to treat his children differently. David was always being praised but Katee never seemed to be able to please her father and often felt his anger.

Perhaps Brian's behaviour had driven Katee into the anorexia?

The thought hit Jane like a bolt of lightning. Could that be why he wouldn't acknowledge Katee's illness? Was he afraid that the doctors would blame him? Jane had blamed herself as soon as she'd heard the doctor's diagnosis and maybe Brian was doing the same thing. She needed to talk to her husband but first of all she wanted to see Katee's doctor.

∞∞∞∞∞

The trip to the hospital was traumatic for both mother and daughter. Katee wanted to be honest with her Mum and share her feelings of confusion and hurt. She wanted to tell her how scared she felt and how chaotic everything had become. She needed to be hugged and reassured that everything was going to be all right. But the anorexia held her back. The 'voice' told her that the only way they'd win was if she kept quiet. If she didn't want to get fat then they had to fight this battle alone and, as always, Katee had listened to the 'voice' and obeyed.

The hospital admission procedure had passed in a blur. A nurse had met them at reception with a porter and a wheelchair. Katee had argued that she could walk to the ward but the nurse had been adamant. The doctor didn't want her exerting herself in any way because it could put too much strain on her heart.

Katee felt humiliated as she was wheeled along the corridors. Why was everyone making such a fuss? There really was nothing wrong with her.

When they reached the Eating Disorders ward, they were greeted by a staff nurse who showed them into a side office.

"Let's do all the paperwork in here so that you can have some privacy," she said, smiling warmly. "Now Katee, I need to ask you a series of questions and then I'll call the doctor who'll do a physical examination."

Katee's stomach lurched. The idea of a physical examination was terrifying. What exactly did it involve? Before she had a chance to ask, she realised the nurse had already asked her first question.

"Katee? Did you hear me? What's your full name?"

The questions seemed to go on forever and by the time they reached the end of the form, Katee felt they knew absolutely everything about her.

"I'm sorry there are so many questions Katee. It just helps the doctors to have a little background information." The nurse apologised while she filed away the form. "Right, next we need to check in your belongings. I'll just fetch another nurse to help me with the list."

Katee watched in amazement as the two nurses unpacked and recorded details of every item in her bag. When they discovered her needlework kit, which contained the three large sharp needles, the staff nurse turned to her.

"Katee, we're going to have to keep this kit at the nurses station because these needles could be dangerous. I'm sorry. I know it must seem a bit harsh that we're taking it away but if you need it then you can always use it in the presence of a nurse."

Katee was stunned. What was this? It felt more like a prison than a hospital.

When the nurses had checked through her bags and listed all her belongings, Katee was asked to sign the form. She felt uncomfortable. By signing, wasn't she going along with them? Wasn't she accepting their treatment? She glared at the nurses as she finally scribbled her name on the line they indicated.

"Thanks Katee. Now let me go and see if the doctor is ready so we can get that physical over and done with."

Katee had momentarily forgotten about the physical in her indignation at having her bags searched.

"Do I have to have a physical? There's nothing wrong with me. There really isn't. My doctor examined me just the other day." Katee spoke quickly and desperately. "So did a doctor here at this hospital last week. You can ask him if you don't believe me. His name is Dr. Elliot."

"It's not that we don't believe you Katee," the nurse replied. "It's just hospital policy. All patients have a physical when they're admitted. The doctor needs to check your weight, height and blood pressure as well as a few other things. It's all very routine and basic and nothing to worry about. In fact, it'll all be over in just a few minutes."

The nurse disappeared and Katee turned to her mother.

"Don't make me go Mum. I'll eat properly again if you just let me come home. Please don't make me stay here. It's horrible."

Again, Jane felt torn and she wished she could take her child's place instead. It was just too painful watching her go through so much distress. She experienced a sudden burst of anger towards Brian. Where was he when they needed him? What gave him the right to desert his family at such a desperate time?

"Oh Katee love, I'd take you home if I could. Please believe me when I say that but the doctors wouldn't let me. You have heart problems and they need to keep an eye on you. I'd never forgive myself if anything happened to you. Tell you what though. How about we think up a special treat for when you come home again? You can choose anything you want. A party or a shopping trip to London. How does that sound?"

Katee shrugged sulkily. Why wouldn't Mum help? She hated her for bringing her to the hospital and wanted to be as difficult as possible but there was also a part of her that needed love. She wanted her Mum to hold her and comfort her. She needed to be told that everything was going to be all right.

Jane felt such sadness as she looked at her daughter. Why had all this happened to their family? If only she could turn back the clock and do things differently so that Katee didn't become ill.

At that moment, the nurse returned to collect Katee and took her down the corridor to a small room at the end. Katee saw a young woman in a white coat standing in front of a desk, writing on a clipboard. The resident doctor looked up as she heard footsteps in the room.

"Hello. You must be Katee. My name is Dr. Carlisle and I need to give you a short examination and then we can finally let you get into bed. It's crazy coming into hospital isn't it? So many people to meet and questions to answer. I'm sure you must be getting tired."

Katee just nodded silently while picking absentmindedly at her fingernails. She and the 'voice' had decided not to make it easy for the doctors.

After a moment of silence, Dr. Carlisle spoke again.

"Okay Katee. Can you slip off your clothes so that you're wearing just your bra and pants?"

Katee glared at the doctor. She wanted to argue because the thought of being seen almost naked was terrifying. She realised though that the doctor would just wait until Katee gave in. She was defeated. Slowly, she started to undress. As she removed each layer of clothing, she felt a growing numbness. Her courage and strength seemed to disappear with her outer garments and she was soon reduced to a small frightened child.

Dr Carlisle knew that her patient was very scared and spoke quietly and gently.

"Let's start with your weight Katee. Can you stand on these scales for me?"

All the fight had gone out of Katee and she stepped slowly onto the large hospital scales. She stared down at her feet and tried to read the scale as the doctor recorded the result. Feeling a sudden panic, she realised that she couldn't understand the strange dial at all. She had to know her weight. The information was just too important to her.

"What's my weight?" she asked frantically.

"Not nearly enough Katee," the doctor replied. "We're going to have to do something about that. Now could you come over here so that I can measure you?"

"But what exactly is my weight?" Katee repeated, slightly louder.

"You should let us worry about that for a while Katee. You're going to just need to concentrate on getting well again."

"But I NEED TO KNOW MY WEIGHT!" Katee shouted in desperation.

A nurse put her head around the door, concerned about the level of noise coming from the clinic. The doctor walked over to the nurse and they spoke quietly for a few minutes. While they were talking, Katee tried to edge closer to the desk where the doctor had left the clipboard which contained a note of her weight. She was nearly close enough to see the figure when the doctor finished her conversation and walked back into the room.

"Sorry about that Katee. Come on. Let's do your height okay?"

Reluctantly, Katee allowed the doctor to carry out the rest of the tests. Her mind was totally preoccupied with her weight and the 'voice' was screaming. She had to find out what she weighed. There had to be a way. She just needed time to think.

When the tests were finished, the doctor allowed Katee to dress again and then asked her to sit on a chair opposite the desk.

"Katee, I couldn't help noticing that you had some cuts on your arms. Would you like to talk to me about them?"

"I had an accident," Katee quickly replied.

"They don't really look like accidental cuts Katee. In fact, they look like you may have done them yourself." Dr. Carlisle lowered her voice. "Many people with eating disorders harm themselves because they feel a lot of self-hatred. Do you ever feel like that?"

"No," Katee said in a tone which indicated that the subject was definitely closed.

"Okay. Well maybe you'll be able to talk a little more with Sally Wilkins when she comes onto the ward tomorrow," Dr. Carlisle suggested. "She's the resident therapist here and will be able to help you work through some of your feelings and anxieties."

Katee just shrugged again. She hated herself for being so difficult but she couldn't talk to the doctor. Her internal 'voice' just wouldn't let her. It had told her to stay silent and that's what she had to do.

Dr. Carlisle realised that Katee was simply too shell-shocked to speak that day and decided to take her back to the ward.

Ten minutes later, Katee was shown to her bed in the corner of the Eating Disorders ward. She looked around and saw that half of the beds were filled with very thin young women. Other girls kept wandering in and out of the room. They would pick up an object from the drawers beside a bed and then leave again. They looked reasonably healthy and Katee wasn't sure if they were patients or visitors. She felt so confused. Everything was so alien. She didn't even know where the bathroom was.

She looked across to the nurses station and saw her mother chatting with the doctor. She hated the way that everyone spoke about her as if she didn't exist. It was humiliating. She wanted to stand on her bed and yell out loud that she had feelings too but then she remembered that the 'voice' didn't want her to speak at all. So once again, she remained silent.

She watched a cheerful nurse walk silently towards her.

Did they always smile? Were they trained at nursing school to keep a permanent grin stuck on their faces? Katee thought angrily. She couldn't remember when she'd last really smiled. Life just felt too hard these days.

"Hi Katee. I'm Liz and I'm a nurse on this ward. I've been assigned to be your key worker, which means that I'll be here to help you in any way I can. If you're struggling to cope with any of your feelings then we can talk about those together."

Katee looked at Liz sadly.

"I don't want to be here," she said quietly.

"I know Katee. Very few people ever want to come into hospital but sometimes it's essential. You're having heart problems because you're eating so little and we need to sort that out."

"But I don't want to eat any more," Katee stated.

"I understand but you see that's one of the symptoms of anorexia. For a while, you're just going to have to trust us because you're not strong enough to look after yourself."

Katee felt her resolve begin to crumble. She really didn't want to like anyone in the hospital but Liz just seemed so kind. She didn't shout like her Dad or ignore her like most of the girls at school did. In fact, she was promising to take over for a while and just let Katee have a break. This idea both relieved and terrified Katee and she let out a little whimper.

"What's on your mind Katee? You sound very sad," Liz asked with concern.

"I don't know anything any more. I can't make myself eat. I feel bad and hateful. I'm so fat and I just wanted to hide but then everyone started making a fuss and said I was too thin. It's like everything's gone out of control."

Katee couldn't believe that she was sharing her thoughts. She'd promised the 'voice' she wouldn't do that. What would it say to her now? What would it dream up as a punishment this time?

Liz saw the confusion and desperation in the girl's face. She'd seen that look a hundred times before and knew about the muddled thoughts that were running through Katee's head. Reaching over, she gently pulled the thin young woman towards her and gave her a hug.

"It'll be okay but you'll need to let us help you. If you fight us then it'll be so much harder."

"But you don't understand. I can't eat. I'm not allowed to," Katee desperately tried to explain.

"You are allowed to Katee. It just feels like you're not. Feelings can be very powerful. You feel fat but the truth is that you're very thin and that's why we need to help you."

Katee listened to the nurse. She could barely hear her words though because the 'voice' was shouting loudly.

"Don't listen to her! I'm the only one that can save you. They want to trick you and make you fat again. DON'T LET THEM TAKE CONTROL!"

Confusion, fear and loneliness swept through Katee and she found herself wanting to scream and cry all at the same time. Liz noticed that Katee had tuned out and gently touched her hand.

"Katee? Katee did you hear me?"

"What's that?" Katee jumped in surprise.

"I was explaining that the doctors will have a meeting tomorrow morning to decide on your treatment plan but for today, we just want you to try and take it easy. I'm going to get you some lunch soon and we'll see how you do with that okay?"

The word 'lunch' sent Katee into a further panic and she barely acknowledged her Mum when she arrived by the bed.

"The nurses have asked me to leave now love," Jane said. "They're going to take care of you for the rest of day but they said I could come and visit tomorrow. I love you sweetheart. I'll be thinking of you all the time. You're very special. Please try to co-operate with the doctors and nurses. Okay?"

Jane bent down to give her daughter a hug but it felt like she was cuddling a stiff board. Katee was away in her own anorexic world and she didn't even feel her mother's arms around her. Jane fought back the swelling tears and fixed a strong and brave smile on her face.

"Take care darling. Remember, I love you."

Katee looked up to see her Mum leaving the ward and felt sadness and loneliness dragging her down once again. What good was the 'voice' now? She wanted her Mum back. She desperately wished she could turn back the clock. If she'd never started dieting maybe she wouldn't be controlled by that damn 'voice' now. It was all her fault. She'd done this to herself. She was the one to blame. Turning her face to the wall and her back to the ward, Katee curled into a ball and started to sob.

25
A Difficult Week

Gemma couldn't believe how the week had just flown by. Such a lot had happened in the last seven days since their first support group meeting. She'd met with Tim on three different occasions and they spoke on the phone nearly every day. She realised that he was becoming a very special part of her life. Melissa was also really important to her now and they were inseparable at school.

Life with her mother had been a little easier since she'd talked with Melissa about her feelings. She didn't feel quite so alone any more. If her Mum shouted at her or left her feeling depressed, Gemma discussed it with Melissa. She'd had only one brief bulimic episode that week and felt intensely proud of the progress she was making.

In fact, the only real disappointment that week was the disappearance of Katee. She hadn't shown up at school on Monday morning and no one knew where she was. Gemma had asked a few teachers but they had been very cagey. They'd said that Katee was fine but wouldn't be in school for a couple of weeks. However much Gemma tried to pry further information out of them, they all kept quiet. It was as if they'd signed a pact of silence. It really was very strange.

∞∞∞∞

Melissa's week had not been quite as good. She had really struggled with her weekly task for the group. She'd chosen not to have any chocolate on Wednesday but it turned out to be harder than she first thought. In fact, from the moment she woke up, all she could think about was chocolate. Walking to school was a nightmare. Every shop she passed seemed to cry out to her to come in and buy chocolate. She felt desperate – like an addict who needed a fix of a drug.

Wednesday morning had been hard but she'd made it through to lunch time without a single bite of chocolate passing her lips. She was beginning to feel a little calmer when something happened to throw her completely off balance. As usual, Cassie was strutting around the school like a peacock, surrounded by her ever-growing band of followers. Melissa had tried to dodge down a side corridor but Caz had spotted her prey and quickly closed in. Melissa actually found herself wondering how someone who wore such high-heeled shoes could move so fast.

Cassie's words had been particularly spiteful that day and Melissa was left feeling disgusting. Self-hatred built in her all afternoon. She felt ashamed of her weight and started to believe Cassie's words. Everyone did hate her. They did all laugh at her behind her back and she was revolting. Instead of finding Gemma so that she could discuss her feelings, Melissa walked out of the school. She'd never skipped a lesson before but she just couldn't face the rest of her class. She slipped out of the basement entrance and slowly walked down to the park.

She had to pass both the newsagent and the grocery store to reach the park. The pride she'd felt at managing a chocolate free morning had disappeared. What was the point in fighting so hard to beat her eating problems when there would always be people like Caz to bring her down? She'd always be considered the 'fat' one at school so why was she even bothering to fight it? She stopped off at the store, stocked up on chocolate bars and took them with her into the park.

As always, Melissa had turned to chocolate to ease her pain for but for the first time ever, it didn't work. Halfway through her third bar of chocolate, she'd stopped. The pain was as bad as ever. The chocolate hadn't buried any of her feelings and Melissa couldn't understand what had happened. She'd thrown the rest of the bars into a bin and wandered over to the lake.

For an hour, she sat and thought about her life. She wondered why the food hadn't helped and suspected it was the therapy that was altering everything. She had a feeling that knowing why she binged on chocolate was the key. Now she understood that it was her way of coping with bad feelings, it no longer worked. Part of her wanted to go back in time so that she could bury her pain beneath food again but part of her felt relieved. Maybe the fact that food was no longer an immediate comfort was good. Maybe she should have tried talking to Gemma first, instead of running away.

Melissa decided she wanted to talk about her experience at the next meeting. That Wednesday night, she'd begun writing a journal so she could keep track of her feelings and emotions. It was hard work because she had to be honest with herself but it was helping her to look at her behaviour. She decided to take the diary with her to that week's meeting. Maybe she'd even be able to read some entries out loud to everyone.

∞∞∞∞

However, of all the three girls, it was Katee who'd had the hardest week of all. For the first three days, she'd been connected to a heart monitor while the doctors checked her heartbeat. She wasn't allowed out of bed and nurses seemed to continually bring her food. All day Sunday, she'd refused every drink and meal.

By Monday lunch time, the nurses were getting desperate and the resident doctor was called. She told Katee that if she wasn't able to eat by herself then they would have to fit a naso-gastric tube. She explained that this was a thin tube they'd insert up her nose, down her throat and into her stomach. They'd then be able to pass food through the tube. Katee had shuddered at the revolting thought of a tube being pushed up her nose and had started to try some food. It was as if her inner 'voice' knew that she had no choice and it left her in peace. Both Katee and the 'voice' realised that if she didn't eat then they would just force calories into her another way.

The first meal had been the hardest of all. She'd picked at a few slices of carrot while Liz sat beside her, encouraging her and telling stories from her own life. Gradually during the week, Katee had started to eat more. She'd forgotten how wonderful food could actually taste. The first time she had a jacket potato topped with cheese was extraordinary. She'd savoured every mouthful. The fluffy potato was laced with creamy butter and the topping of grated cheese was piping hot and melting. She couldn't admit to the staff that she was enjoying the food though. She could barely admit it to herself. The 'voice' wanted her to believe that food was evil.

As the days passed, Katee found herself secretly looking forward to meal times. At nine o'clock in the morning, a nurse brought around a menu and helped the patients choose their meals for the day. Katee loved this time. She revelled in looking down the list to see which meal she would have that day. It had been months since she'd been allowed to eat but now she had no choice. She kept repeating the phrase over and over to herself – I have no choice. It was those few words that kept the guilt at bay.

By Thursday, the doctors believed that Katee was ready to see the therapist for the first time. They'd taken her off the monitor that morning as her heart rate had finally returned to a regular pattern. For the first time since she'd arrived, Katee was able to get up and walk around the ward. Liz took her on a guided tour and introduced her to all the other patients who were on bed-rest. She'd asked if they all had heart problems and Liz had explained that these patients were just too underweight to even move. Until they gained some weight, their lives were in danger if they did just the smallest amount of exercise.

Katee had felt shocked when she'd heard Liz's answer. She really hadn't thought it was possible to become so ill just because you didn't eat enough. She desperately wanted to ask if they all had an inner 'voice' that controlled the way they behaved but she was still too afraid. She was certain that the doctors would think she was crazy if she spoke of a 'voice' in her head, so she stayed quiet. The 'voice' congratulated her.

Her first meeting with Sally Wilkins had been interesting, although Katee would never have admitted this fact either. Sally had spent an hour with her and had chatted generally about anorexia, self-harming and therapy. She'd explained that she would see Katee every day while she was an in-patient but the therapy would also continue when she was discharged. Sally would set up weekly appointments so that she could help Katee learn to understand why she'd become anorexic in the first place and how to cope in the future.

Sally had also told Katee about the weekly support group. She suggested that Katee joined Liz and the other three girls from the unit that week when they walked down to the meeting. The idea of being in a roomful of people terrified Katee. She'd become quite used to the enclosed ward that was quiet for most of the day. She certainly didn't feel that she could face fourteen adults all staring at her. Sally had explained that two new girls had joined the previous week and she wouldn't be the only nervous one there but Katee was still unsure.

It was actually the 'voice' who made the final decision. Katee was still confined to the ward on the third floor but the support group was held in a room on the second floor. Walking to the meeting would only burn off a few calories but the 'voice' told Katee it was a start.

On Friday morning, Katee told Liz that she would like to join the group and she saw immediate delight on her key worker's face.

"That's great Katee," Liz enthused. "I'm sure you'll enjoy it. It's really informal. Everyone's very friendly and did Sally tell you that we have some new girls too?"

Katee nodded and smiled shyly. She liked Liz. She'd even been able to tell her a few of her anorexic secrets. Liz had listened carefully but hadn't pushed her to tell more. It was as if she knew that Katee needed to take it at her own pace.

Saturday passed quickly for Katee. There were no doctors on duty, which meant no ward rounds. Visitors were allowed all day and some of the patients even went home on leave. Katee spent the whole afternoon with her Mum.

When she arrived at the ward, Jane immediately noticed a difference in her daughter. There was some colour in her cheeks and her eyes didn't look quite so lifeless. She was also pretty sure that she'd even seen the flicker of a smile when she entered the room.

Katee had promised the 'voice' that she would give her mother a hard time when she visited. It had whispered instructions at her all morning.

"It's your Mum's fault you're in here you know? If she hadn't taken you to the doctor's in the first place, you'd still be at home. You have to be really horrible to her or else you'll be in here forever!"

For the first few minutes, Katee had tried to blank her Mum but she'd been too excited to have a visitor. The hospital had allowed Jane to visit the first night but had then suggested it might be better for Katee if she didn't return until the weekend. Katee needed to settle in and too many visits could be disruptive. This had been very hard on Katee though, especially as some of the other patients were allowed regular visitors.

Jane chatted for a while about her week and how everything was at home. Katee had just listened at first but within five minutes, she started to talk about how her own week had been. Jane thought it was wonderful to see her daughter more animated and alive.

Katee chatted for half an hour until Jane realised she could put it off no longer. She had to mention Brian. He hadn't even returned home until Wednesday. Jane didn't know where he'd been or what he'd done but he was still wearing the same set of clothes and had a four-day beard. She realised that he was struggling with Katee's illness and so it was Jane who eventually had to bring the subject up with him.

She had stood transfixed in amazement when she saw her husband suddenly burst into tears and sob uncontrollably. Astonished, she realised that she'd never actually seen Brian cry. He'd always just shown anger whenever he felt upset or worried. Jane remained silent and in short, stuttering sentences Brian began to talk.

He explained that he'd never really known how to treat Katee when she became a teenager. He wanted her to succeed at school because he knew that his lack of qualifications had held him back but perhaps he'd gone too far. Maybe he'd pushed her just a bit too hard. Lately, he'd found that he hadn't been able to control his temper and had even started lashing out at her. He was scared. He didn't like the person he'd become but he didn't know how to change.

Jane had tried to encourage him to go down to the hospital to talk with Katee and the doctors but he refused. He felt too ashamed to face his daughter. Jane explained that he could join her and Katee in family therapy. She told him that no one would judge him but this terrified him even more. The thought of doctors sitting and analysing his behaviour frightened him so much that he felt the anger rising in him again.

Storming out of the house once more, he disappeared for another night and when he finally returned on Thursday, he was denying his feelings again. He wouldn't even discuss what had been said on Wednesday evening and Jane felt hopeless. It was as if she'd been allowed a brief glimpse of the husband she used to know but then he'd been snatched away from her again.

She'd asked the doctors what she should tell Katee about Brian's behaviour and they'd encouraged her to be as honest as possible. They had explained that the lack of communication in their family could have contributed to Katee's problems developing to such a dangerous level.

Calmly and carefully, Jane started to describe the events from that week. She saw the fear and confusion appear in Katee's eyes as soon as she mentioned Brian's name. Katee allowed her mother to reach the end of her story before she said anything and then she spoke with a passion that shocked Jane.

"I hate him Mum. Why couldn't he be like other people's Dads? Why couldn't he just love me for who I am? Why do I have to achieve so much and make up for his mistakes? I don't want to see him again."

Jane could understand her daughter's feelings. She'd experienced many similar emotions herself during the last few days.

"I think we just have to be patient honey. I think in time your father will want to join us in family therapy and then we can all talk honestly together."

"Well if he goes to family therapy then I won't," Katee said defiantly.

"Oh love, don't be like that. You have to give your Dad a chance," Jane said, trying to placate her daughter.

"Why? He hasn't given me one."

"I know but remember his parents were very strict and they really didn't allow him to talk about his feelings. He grew up thinking it was somehow wrong to show his emotions. It's as if all those feelings that he tried to bury have suddenly risen to the surface and he just can't handle them."

"I guess I can sort of understand that Mum," Katee said very quietly. "I feel that's happening to me. I can't control the way I feel any more. I'll be thinking that I'm fine and then suddenly I get so sad that I just start crying. It's scary. Maybe that's how Dad feels."

"I think it is love and remember that as an adult man, he feels he has to be strong for his whole family. Losing his job just left him feeling a complete failure and like he'd let us all down."

Katee went quiet for a minute.

"I need space Mum. Maybe I don't hate Dad but I still don't want to see him yet. You won't make me will you?"

Jane knew she had to support her daughter. She felt so divided. She wanted to look after both Brian and Katee at once but she knew who came first right now. They hadn't given Katee enough of their time or love recently and all that mattered was getting her better. She nodded and smiled.

"We'll take everything at a pace you can manage sweetheart. You just concentrate on getting well."

Jane left at five o'clock as the nurses started to serve tea. Katee was then occupied with her meal until half past six, when Liz walked over and sat down beside her bed.

"So, are you still coming down to the group tonight?"

"Hmmmm…yeah," Katee said distractedly.

"You sound a bit upset Katee. Did everything go okay with your Mum?"

"I guess it did, but she told me some stuff about my Dad… "

"Do you want to talk about it?" Liz enquired gently.

"No. I want to think."

"Okay, well remember that you can always talk to me. Maybe when you've had time to think about what your Mum said, we can have a chat. You may even feel like sharing some thoughts at the group tonight."

Katee looked at Liz as if she was mad.

Yeah right. Like that would happen.

She didn't want to go to the meeting at all and was only going for the exercise. She certainly wasn't going to speak.

They really didn't get it did they?

"Okay Katee," Liz replied. "Well I've got to collect the other girls. I'll be back for you in a few minutes so get yourself ready. You'll need some shoes as we're leaving the ward."

Katee watched her walk away. What was it that held her back from opening up to people like Liz? Part of her had really wanted to share her thoughts. Why did she always have to push people away?

∞∞∞∞

Gemma and Melissa felt more comfortable arriving for their second group meeting. They greeted Sandra, Jeff and Jan as if they'd known them for weeks. Melissa asked Jeff how his week had been and Gemma chatted to Jan about her dental appointments. At seven o'clock, Liz walked in with the girls from the Eating Disorders ward.

"I think I'll go and say hello this time." Gemma said, turning to Melissa. "We don't get a chance to speak to them after the meeting like we do with everyone else."

Halfway across the room Gemma stopped dead, frozen in her tracks. Liz had brought four girls with her this week and when she moved aside to let them into the room, Gemma found herself staring directly into the eyes of Katee Quinn.

26
The Discovery

Katee was just as shocked as Gemma. She stood and stared as Gemma slowly walked towards her and began to speak.

"Katee…Hi. Whoa…I didn't expect to see you here. We've really missed you at school this week but none of the teachers would tell us where you were. Are you…okay?"

"Yeah…I'm fine but nobody will believe that," Katee replied bitterly.

Gemma was just about to ask Katee why she had been admitted to the hospital when Sally called the meeting to order and she had to quickly scurry back to her seat next to Melissa. Katee felt even more surprised when she saw that Melissa was at the meeting as well.

Why were they both here? she thought uneasily. Had they been sent to spy on her?

The meeting began in the same way as before, with everyone introducing themselves. Katee very quietly muttered a short introduction.

"I'm Katee and I don't really know why I'm here. I guess I had some heart problems or something."

Gemma wasn't really any the wiser as to why Katee had joined the meeting but she guessed that a doctor had finally diagnosed anorexia.

Sally thanked Katee for her contribution and asked everyone to talk about their week.

Melissa listened carefully while Jan, Jeff and Simone spoke. Simone hadn't contributed to the group before and Melissa found her speech very moving. She felt close to tears as the young woman described her painful childhood and how worthless she had always felt. It must have been really hard for her to share such personal information and suddenly Melissa knew that she wanted to speak too. She started shyly.

"I'd like to thank Simone for saying all that she just did. Sorry. I don't know if you usually thank people but it meant a lot to me and if it's alright, I'd like to share something too."

Melissa turned to Sally to check that it was okay to speak.

"Of course you can share Melissa," Sally reassured her. "And it's always nice when people say if something has helped them. We often talk about how hard issues are for us but forget to say when someone or something has helped."

Melissa nodded with interest. Sally was right. It was much easier to focus on how bad you felt all the time. Did she even pay attention to the times when she felt happy? Maybe she was afraid to acknowledge when she was happy, in case it jinxed the feeling and made it disappear.

Sally continued speaking.

"Do you still want to share Melissa or have you changed your mind? It's okay either way."

"Oh, I'm sorry. I was thinking about what you just said. Erm…what I wanted to share was about Wednesday and the task I picked out last week, which was to go a whole day without chocolate. I didn't manage to do it and something really weird happened to me." Melissa paused and drew a deep breath. Sharing her feelings was hard. She felt shaky and her palms were wet with sweat. She explained about her afternoon and the incident at the park.

"…so I guess I realised that because I now know what I use the chocolate for…you know, to bury my feelings…it doesn't work any more."

"That's very interesting Melissa," Sally replied. "Can you tell us how that made you feel?"

"Er…well…um…I can actually 'cause I started to write a journal on Wednesday night so that I wouldn't forget my feelings."

"Would you like to read us a little Melissa?"

"Okay but…er…I'm not a writer or anything, so it may be kind of rough."

Melissa wiped her hands on her skirt and reached into her bag. Pulling out a small notebook with a picture of a cartoon dog on the front, she turned to the first page.

"Okay. Here goes…

Today was tough. Cassie was really horrible to me at school and then I did a really bad thing. I just walked out between classes and went to the park. I bought loads of chocolate on the way and pigged out but it didn't stop the pain. It wasn't chocolate I needed, it was someone to talk to and I realised I should have shared my feelings with Gemma. I sat by the lake and felt such a failure. I've messed up so much of my life. Gemma and the new support group are the only things I feel good about. I hate my size, I hate being so scared all the time and I hate Cassie bullying me.

…erm…that's all I wrote," Melissa finished.

Sally looked impressed.

"It's very good Melissa and I'm really glad you shared it with us. Can I ask you a question?"

"Sure."

"Why did you choose to cut out chocolate for a whole day?"

Melissa was surprised by the question.

"Oh…well…I thought it would be good for me. Chocolate's a bad food and I pig out on it and I thought it'd be the right thing to do."

"Okay, does anyone want to help Melissa with her thoughts here?"

Sandra nervously started to speak.

"I have a feeling I know what Sally's getting at here because I did the same thing when I first joined the group. If I'm right, it's about 'bad' foods and 'good' foods. Is that it Sally?"

"Absolutely Sandra. Go ahead and share your thoughts with Melissa."

"Right, well my first task for my first group was to not eat any 'bad' foods that might trigger a binge but Sally explained that no food should be considered 'bad'. All foods are okay and it's just about getting the proportions right. Do you know what I'm saying? If you try to cut out a food or make it forbidden then it's going to become even more appealing. What you need to do is allow yourself some chocolate every day so that it isn't just a binge food for when you feel bad."

Sally thanked Sandra and then turned to Melissa.

"Does that make sense?"

"Yeah I guess…but isn't chocolate really bad for you?"

"It sure is." Kim spoke up for the first time during the meeting. "It contains zillions of calories."

"No, Kim it doesn't contain 'zillions of calories,'" Sally patiently replied. "It does in fact contain certain nutrients that are very good for us, such as calcium and iron. If you eat it in moderate amounts, it can be a lovely treat."

"Yeah right," Kim said sarcastically.

Sally spoke quietly and calmly.

"Remember Kim that food is an essential part of life. When you start limiting it then in time you're going to start damaging your body. Food is like oxygen. It's vital for us. Would you limit the amount of oxygen you breathe just because you felt it was 'bad' to breathe?"

Kim looked down at the floor and didn't answer. Sally gave the group a few moments to absorb what she'd said and then turned back to Melissa.

"So what should I have chosen as a task Sally?" Melissa asked.

"Well it's always important to take small steps when you're trying to beat an addiction or an eating disorder of any kind. If you try to take on too much then there's the chance you won't succeed and that'll leave you feeling even more of a failure."

"I must admit…" Melissa said in a voice that was barely audible. "…I did feel nervous about coming today because I knew I'd failed my task and was sure everyone else would have done much better."

"How about trying something different, like working on your feelings about yourself?" Sally suggested. "Could your task for next week be to write a list of things that you do like about yourself? We all understand that you feel bad about yourself but how about looking for some things that you like?"

Melissa nodded. She liked the idea of that task although she had a feeling it was going to be very hard.

"Thanks for sharing that with us Melissa," Sally said, turning to Gemma. "Now Gemma, how did you get on with your first task?"

Gemma swallowed nervously and heard her voice crack as she started to speak. She cleared her throat and began again.

"I think I did okay last week. In fact it was a pretty good week all round. I…um…I've got a new boyfriend called Tim and I managed to tell him about my bulimia." As Gemma said the word bulimia, there was an audible gasp. Glancing around, she saw that Katee had a look of horror and amazement on her face. Gemma's face flushed with embarrassment and she stopped speaking.

"Is everything alright Katee?" Sally asked.

"Oh…erm…ah…yeah…I'm so sorry I didn't mean to make a noise. Gemma I'm sorry. I didn't know you had bulimia. I didn't mean to be rude. I'm sorry."

Katee's face was now as red as Gemma's and she stared down at her feet.

"Do you two know each other?" Sally enquired with interest.

"Yeah they do," Melissa answered. "Katee's in our class at school and she'd just joined our group, if you know what I mean, before she had to…er…before she was absent for a few days."

"Wow. It must have been quite a surprise when you all met up here. Are you okay about that?" Sally asked. "Do you want to have a little meeting of your own after the group ends? I'm sure Liz wouldn't mind Katee having an extra ten minutes away from the ward."

The three girls looked at each other and started nodding. Katee spoke up first.

"That would be good."

"Great," said Sally. "Okay, Gemma do you want to continue?"

Gemma briefly described her week and finished by talking about her Mum.

"It was weird but she didn't upset me as much this week. She still kept comparing me to her and telling me that I wasn't ever going to get anywhere but it didn't hurt as much. Although I'm not really sure why."

"Well Gemma, maybe it's because you now have Tim in your life. You can see by his reaction to you that your Mum's words might not be true. He's putting some doubts in your head. In the past, you've always believed everything she said but now you have someone who's telling you something different. The fact that he's boosting your self-esteem outweighs her comments that lower it."

"Whoa, yeah. I guess that does make sense."

Sally paused. "Do you want to try and take a risk this week Gemma?"

"Erm…I dunno. Is it going to be really difficult?" Gemma replied nervously.

"Well you can take it at your own pace really. What I would like you to do is try and explain some of your feelings to your Mum."

Gemma felt shocked. She didn't know whether or not she had enough courage to talk with her Mum yet.

"I'm not sure Sally. I mean…will it really help? My Mum's so certain that she's right all the time."

"Do you know Gemma, a lot of people who seem very definite and forceful actually have insecurities of their own," Sally explained. "Low self-esteem can show itself in many different ways. A need to be powerful and control others through hurtful words or behaviour often shows underlying self-esteem problems."

Gemma had a look of deep concentration on her face.

"Hmmm. I see. But why would my Mum have low self-esteem though? She's got a good job, she makes a lot of money, she's got loads of qualifications, she's pretty and she's thin."

"Yes but do you think that there's anything lacking in your mother's life Gemma? Do you think she feels there's anything she failed at?"

Gemma paused again to think about the question. As she pondered on her answer, a very quiet and timid voice spoke up.

"I think my Dad's like your Mum Gemma," Katee said.

"He gets at me a lot and tries to control me. I never get good enough grades. I'm not pretty enough or thin enough for him. I just thought that it was because I was such a horrible person and it probably is but…erm…he…um…he also lost his job about a year ago and maybe he feels a failure?" Katee's voice trailed away as she reached the end of her sentence.

Sally listened intently to the new speaker. Katee Quinn was obviously very intelligent but sadly she was punishing herself for another person's problems.

"Katee, thanks for speaking to the group. I know it's hard to join in at your first meeting. It does sound as though your Dad and Gemma's Mum could be quite similar. Gemma, have you remembered anything about your Mum that could make her feel like a failure?"

"Well…er…yeah. When Katee said about her Dad, I remembered of course that I don't really have a Dad. He walked out on us when I was still little because he just couldn't cope with how bossy my Mum was. Maybe she feels a failure because of that? She's always telling me that it's my fault he left but that just doesn't seem right. He still phones me at times but he never speaks to her." Gemma was feeling angry by the time she reached the end of her last sentence.

"That's very interesting Gemma," Sally replied. "It sounds as though both you and Katee have parents that can't cope with their own feelings of inadequacy. This is quite common but it's not right that they take it out on you. Nobody should ever have to accept bad treatment or cruelty. It's important that, in time, you learn to separate yourself from your parents behaviour."

"But I can't leave home," Katee said in a panicked voice.

Sandra was sitting beside Katee and could feel the girl begin to shake. Gently putting her own hand over Katee's, she spoke with understanding.

"Sally's not suggesting you do that hon but she's saying you need to distance yourself emotionally. That's really hard to do and I know because I've been trying to do it myself. You feel like you're getting somewhere and think that you're not affected so much by your Mum or Dad and then…WHAM!" Sandra slapped her free hand hard on her leg, making the whole group jump. "They say something that sends you right back into a spiral. But you have to pick yourself up and start again." Sandra stopped speaking and looked desperately to Sally. "I don't think I'm explaining this well."

"You're doing great Sandra," Sally enthused. "It's a tough concept but I know that if Katee continues to come to the group, we can explain it in more detail through our own experiences. Has anyone got an example they'd like to share?"

There was a moment of silence while the members of the group shuffled in their seats, crossing and uncrossing their legs to cover their awkwardness. Finally, Kim spoke up.

"My Dad's like Katee's and he used to shout at me a lot if I annoyed him. It really hurt and I spent all my time trying to please him but I never could, so I stopped eating. I just hated myself so much, I wanted to disappear."

"That's exactly how I feel," Katee almost shouted in amazement. "But what do you do about it?"

"Well the first thing I had to do was tell my doctor how I felt because I was trying to deal with everything the wrong way. I do understand that starving myself doesn't help but I'm stuck and just can't eat, which is why I'm here. While I am here though, the docs are arranging for my Dad to come to family therapy so's we can all talk. And I'm also learning that if he shouts at me then that's his stuff and I don't have to hurt myself coz of his bad behaviour. Like Sandra says, it's real hard but I think I'll get there. I don't want to be ill forever. I want my life back. I want to be happy again."

As she finished her final sentence, the whole group burst into spontaneous applause. The speech was a long one for Kim, who'd previously only ever spoken briefly but more importantly it showed a sense of spirit. Kim had reached rock bottom but was slowly on her way up and everyone in the room felt proud of her achievements.

Sally smiled at the group. There were times when she felt a sense of wonderment at how brave the people surrounding her actually were. They had all experienced troubles in their lives but were now learning how to deal with them healthily. Looking down at her watch, she realised they'd already run five minutes over time.

"Well everyone, it's time I closed this meeting or else we'll be here all night. Gemma, did that help a little?"

"Yeah, it was good thanks. I want to think about Mum and if there's a way I can say a little of what I'm feeling to her. And I want to try to not let her words hurt me so much. I'm going to see if I can listen to Tim instead."

"Great Gemma," Sally replied with enthusiasm. "That's a really good start. Okay, to end the meeting let's all go once round very quickly, picking a task for the upcoming week."

Ten minutes later, the group ended and Katee scuttled over to speak with Gemma and Melissa.

"I was really amazed to see you here," Katee said. "I thought I was dreaming at first. I'm so sorry if it seemed like I was staring Gemma. I just couldn't believe you had eating problems too. You just seem…so together like. Do you know what I mean Melissa?" Katee desperately turned to her for confirmation. Melissa grinned.

"I said exactly the same thing when she first told me about the bulimia. But Katee what are you doing here? Can you tell us?"

Katee paused and looked down.

"Oh sorry. That was the wrong thing to say wasn't it?" Melissa remarked quietly.

"No Mel it wasn't," Katee replied. "I realised today that I have to start being more honest. I was really sure that I would hate this group and not say a thing but I just found myself being drawn in and…you know…I actually feel a bit better because I talked about my Dad. I don't know but I think I want to talk with you more about it. But not here. Not now. I need to think."

"How about we come and visit tomorrow?" Gemma asked.

"Yeah," Melissa added. "We could come in the afternoon and stay for as long as you want."

Katee smiled shyly.

"You'd do that for me? You'd give up your Sunday afternoon to visit a hospital?"

"We're not visiting the hospital, dummy." Gemma grinned. "We're visiting a friend."

Katee's eyes lit up. It felt wonderful to know there were two people that she could actually call her friends. For that moment, even the 'voice' seemed a little quieter. Could it actually be going away?

After ten minutes of chatting, Liz walked over.

"Katee, we have to go back to the ward. Kim's due one of her drinks and she's starting to feel panicked."

"Okay Liz I'm coming," Katee answered. She turned to Gemma and Melissa and said with a big smile: "See you tomorrow then?"

The two girls nodded and smiled in agreement and Katee felt a spark of excitement run down her spine. It really had been quite an amazing meeting. Slowly climbing the stairs with Liz, Katee thought about some of the comments that had been made during the meeting. She recalled Kim and Sandra's words and knew that she wasn't the only one who struggled with a difficult parent.

For the first time in months, Katee relaxed a little and started to think back to her conversation with Gemma and Melissa. Then, as sudden as a flash of lightning across the sky, the 'voice' crashed back into her head.

"You FAILED me! I told you not to talk to anyone. How could you do that? You WILL be punished. I am the ONLY one in control! You cannot live without me. You WILL obey me!"

Liz noticed the colour drain from Katee's face and reached out just in time to catch the young woman as she fell to the floor in a dead faint.

27
A Pact Between Friends

By nine o'clock on Saturday night, Katee was lying in her bed sipping very slowly at a drink. Liz was sitting beside her looking concerned.

"Is there anything you want to tell me?" Liz enquired.

"Like what?" Katee questioned defensively.

"Well, maybe about how you felt just before you fainted. Did you feel dizzy or weak? Maybe going to the group was too much for you."

"No!" Katee snapped. The last thing she wanted was to be banned from going to the group. "I didn't get dizzy."

"Okay, well if it wasn't a physical thing and the docs did say you checked out okay…"

The doctors had spent half an hour doing physical checks and talking with Katee but they'd come up with nothing to explain her sudden faint. Liz had been asked to see if she could discover anything further.

"…maybe it's an emotional problem. Did the group trigger some memories that were painful?"

Katee felt frightened. The 'voice' had amazed her. Its power had been overwhelming and she wasn't sure how to cope any more. She desperately wanted to talk to Liz but the 'voice' was still yelling loud and clear in her head.

"Something like that yeah," Katee almost whispered.

"Can you tell me anything about it?" Liz gently enquired.

Katee was starting to get fed-up. Why wouldn't everyone just leave her alone? She needed some time and space to think about the meeting and she had to make some promises to the 'voice'.

"Can't you just go away Liz? I want some space," she snapped again. "Just leave me ALONE! I can't tell you about the 'voice' okay?"

Katee gasped when she realised what she'd just said. She raised her hands to her face and covered her mouth in horror. She felt an icy finger of fear run down her spine. What had she done?

Very quietly and calmly, Liz spoke.

"Does the 'voice' tell you not to eat Katee?"

"How do you know that?" Katee questioned sharply.

"Does it also tell you that you're fat and don't deserve food?"

"What is this? How do you know what the 'voice' says? Tell me how do you know?" Katee shouted.

"I know about your 'voice' because a lot of people with anorexia feel they hear a 'voice' in their head that controls their behaviour."

"They do?" Katee sounded astonished.

"Yeah they do," Liz continued. "Some people don't really see it as a 'voice' but just think of it as another set of thoughts that continually play in their head. Other people see it more like a little devil that sits on their shoulder telling them not to eat. Some even feel that their body has been totally taken over by the illness."

"Really? Do you mean that?" Katee could not believe what she was hearing. "But…but…I thought if I told you about hearing a 'voice', you'd think I was nuts and the doctors would lock me away."

"You're not crazy Katee. This 'voice' is just part of the illness. We can actually help you to learn how to fight back at it so that it doesn't control you any longer."

"But I don't think I want to lose the 'voice.'" Katee suddenly felt doubtful. "You see…it's helping me to get thin."

"There's a secret about the 'voice' that you don't know yet Katee," Liz said patiently. "The truth is, it only ever lies to you. It tells you that you're fat when the truth is you're really thin. It tells you not to eat when you desperately need food and it tells you not to listen to the doctors. Do you want to trust something that always lies to you?"

"I have to think," Katee said sharply and placed her hands over her ears. "I'm not going to listen to you. The 'voice' is mine and you're just jealous." Hot tears started to sting Katee's eyes but she fought them back. "I want to be left alone for a while. Please go Liz," she begged.

"Okay Katee. I'll leave you in peace but you know where I am if you need me. I'm on duty until ten tonight."

Katee watched Liz walk out of sight. She wanted to call her back so that she could apologise for shouting. She hated herself when she got angry but she really had no control. It wasn't actually her getting angry, it was the 'voice'. Liz didn't understand. It just wasn't possible to fight it. The 'voice' ruled her life.

∞∞∞∞

Gemma and Tim met at midday on Sunday for an early lunch. They'd arranged to join Melissa at the hospital at two o'clock but wanted some time alone first. They had discovered a cosy tea shop near the hospital and were settled into a little corner. Tim had ordered a selection of sandwiches and small cakes and Gemma was carefully sampling the food. She liked the way that Tim would order an assortment of food and just let her choose. She didn't feel pressured to eat a full meal and so would find herself trying some of the goodies she usually just thought of as 'binge' foods.

She had done well on her task the week before and had tried some cake for the first time in four months. The more she heard Sally and the others talking, the more she realised that her diet wasn't healthy. All it had really done for her was cause her to start bingeing, which had led to the vomiting. It had now been seven days since she had last vomited and she was feeling a small amount of pride about her achievement.

"So tell me how the meeting went," Tim asked. "If you want to of course…you don't have to Gemmy…I'm not trying to be nosy."

Gemma loved the way that Tim had already given her a cute nickname. No one had ever called her 'Gemmy' before. Her Dad used to call her 'Gem' or 'kitten' but that was different.

"No, it's cool talking about it. It was such a shock when Katee walked in. I mean, I guess I should have suspected she might have been in hospital 'cause of her anorexia but…Anyway, yeah it was a good meeting but they sort of left me with a tough task."

"Task? What task?" Tim queried.

"Oh yeah, sorry. I guess I'm already getting used to the way the group works." Gemma explained the task system and then told him about hers for that week.

"How am I ever going to talk to my Mum, Tim?"

"Well, what about trying to do it in stages? I'm happy to come with you if you want."

"Hmm. That's really tempting but I think I have to do this alone. It's just…I can feel myself putting it off forever."

"Well, what about setting yourself a time? How about when you get home tonight?"

"Urgh! I s'pose I could but what would I tell her?"

"I don't know much about psychology and stuff but I think if you make out that you're blaming your Mum, she's going to get angry. She might get really defensive, if you know what I mean?"

"Omigod yeah. My Mum is so defensive if you question her about anything." Gemma rolled her eyes at Tim.

"How about starting by asking her how she is?" Tim suggested. "Maybe even tell her that you love her. If you do that is. And then say that it hurts when she criticises you all the time. Say that you do your best but her words often leave you feeling inadequate. Ask her if she's ashamed of you maybe?"

"Whoa! That's difficult stuff to talk about. It sounds very…confrontational," Gemma replied nervously.

"I know Gemmy but maybe you need to try. You know, none of this is going to feel easy. It's a really difficult subject to bring up and talk about."

"Hmmmm." Gemma thought about what Tim had said for a minute as she chewed slowly on a dainty sandwich.

"I'm scared of her Tim," she admitted. "I hate it when she shouts at me. I feel like a little kid again. Like I'm only four years old. Why does she do that to me?"

"Well I think we all feel kind of intimidated by our parents. I know I do. But the thing is that they've looked after us since we were born. And now everything's changing. You're becoming an adult and want to make your own decisions but it's hard because you feel your Mum's still in control."

"Wow that's impressive. How did you learn all this stuff?" Gemma asked.

"It's not that clever really, I just read it in a book. Two years ago, I was having major clashes with my Dad all the time. He wanted to run my life. He wanted to dictate which classes I took for 'A' level. There was this one really major argument when I told him that I was taking psychology.

He went ballistic and said that I could never be a lawyer with such a stupid qualification. He didn't even care that I never had any plans to become a lawyer."

"How are things now Tim?"

"We've kind of reached a truce. He's not happy with what I'm doing and makes a lot of sly digs about my year out but I just have to ignore it. I can't let my parents rule my life forever. It's not healthy, you know? I'm an adult now and I have to make my own decisions."

"You know they were saying that at the group yesterday. Something about putting a special kind of distance…erm…" Gemma paused as she thought. "I got it…'emotional distance' between yourself and your parents." A sudden thought crossed Gemma's mind. "Hey, d'you know that Katee's Dad really shouts at her?"

"That makes a lot of sense," Tim replied.

"Why?"

"Same reason. He shouts, so she feels like a failure and maybe that brought on the anorexia."

"What? So my Mum putting me down could maybe have led me to start bingeing and stuff?"

"Yeah. Maybe."

They talked intensely for nearly two hours before the waitress asked them if they wanted anything else. After paying the bill, they realised they had only five minutes left to get to the hospital.

Tim reached for Gemma's hand and as they walked together, she glowed with happiness. She was still finding it hard to believe that Tim wanted to spend time with her. It was almost as if she was waiting for the bubble to burst. Good things just didn't usually happen to her.

"I think I should wait outside while you and Melissa talk with Katee," Tim decided.

"Oh Tim, I wanted you to meet Katee." Gemma sounded disappointed.

"That's sweet but think about it. She's in hospital and she'll be frightened. She's not going to feel like meeting a total stranger. If she asks to meet me then that's fine but I'll just stay out of sight at first, so's not to embarrass her."

"Okay. It's just I feel…well…kind of proud of you and I wanted to show you off." Gemma blushed as she spoke.

Tim stopped walking and turned to Gemma.

"Hey, you really feel proud of me? That's so cute."

Gemma's face blushed an even deeper red.

"Well yeah I've…um…never really had a boyfriend before. Not that I'm saying you have to be my boyfriend. I mean, when I said 'boyfriend' I'm not saying 'boyfriend boyfriend' but really sort of…a friend who's…a boy." Gemma spoke at a tremendous speed, stammering as she did so. When she reached the end of her sentence she was a dark crimson red.

Tim smiled.

"Gemmy, I loved it that you said I was your boyfriend. Will you be my girlfriend?"

Barely able to believe what she was hearing, Gemma felt swept along by a torrent of emotions.

"Me? You want…me as your girlfriend?"

Placing his hands on her shoulders, Tim bent his head and kissed Gemma softly on the lips.

"Yes please."

∞∞∞∞

Gemma was still glowing when she and Tim met Melissa in the hospital car park. Melissa didn't immediately notice just how happy her friend was though. She was struggling with different emotions and was feeling quite sad.

She had tried to speak with her Mum that morning about some of her eating problems but it hadn't gone well. Her Mum had tried to listen but she just didn't seem to understand. Melissa had explained that she needed to learn how to eat a healthier diet. She had even suggested that she should visit the doctor so that he could refer her to a dietician. Her Mum had just laughed.

"Oh Melly, you're so young. It's years before you need to worry about your health. Enjoy yourself. There'll be plenty of time for strict diets when you're my age."

"But Mum," Melissa said in frustration. "If you and Dad had taken more care when you were my age, you wouldn't be struggling with so many health problems now. I don't want to get diabetes or have a heart attack and I don't want to keep stuffing my face."

Mrs. March had started to become annoyed.

"Nobody's asking you to stuff your face Melly but diets just cause obsessions. We don't want you turning into an anorexic."

At that point, Melissa had also become angry.

"Mum, one of my best friends is anorexic and it's a serious illness you know. It starts for lots of different reasons. It's not just a diet gone wrong."

"There's no need to shout at me missy," Mrs. March had finally said before gathering up her needlework and stomping out of the lounge.

Melissa had immediately felt annoyed with herself for upsetting her Mum. Why had she handled the situation so badly? What could she have said or done differently? She'd been pondering these questions all morning but still hadn't come up with any answers. She smiled bleakly at Gemma.

"Hi Gemma. How you doing?"

"Great. Erm…Melissa, this is my boyfriend Tim. Tim, this is my best friend Melissa." Beaming at them both, Gemma waved her arms in the air as she introduced her two special friends to each other.

Shyly, Tim and Melissa smiled and shook hands as they mumbled brief 'hellos'.

"I think we ought to get up to the ward Gemma," Melissa suggested. "Katee will be waiting for us."

Gemma nodded and turned to Tim.

"Where are you going to wait Tim? Outside the Eating Disorders ward or down in reception?"

Tim decided that reception was best, in case Katee noticed him upstairs. Smiling at Gemma, he squeezed her hand to say good-bye and good luck. As the two girls walked to the lift, Gemma noticed that Melissa was unusually quiet.

"Was it wrong of me to bring Tim? I don't want to upset you Mel. You're really important to me."

"No no Gemma. It's great to meet Tim. It's not him. It's something else. I'm having problems with my Mum and I don't know what to do."

"You wanna tell me?" Gemma asked.

"Yeah but later. We mustn't be late for Katee."

"Okay but I won't forget," Gemma said with concern. "You're not going to hide it away again. Right?"

Melissa couldn't help but smile. It really was quite special having someone around who cared.

As they reached the Eating Disorders ward, the girls fell silent. They were both remembering their first trip there and the shock they'd felt. When they reached reception, they asked for Katee Quinn and were directed to her bed. It was frightening to see how sad their friend looked, hunched up alone on her bed. She was staring distantly into space and Gemma felt she could see waves of emotion crossing her face.

As they approached the bed, both Gemma and Melissa realised Katee had not even seen them. Giving a small cough, Gemma announced their presence. Katee turned to look in their direction and a sad flicker of a smile hovered fleetingly around her mouth.

"Hey. It's so cool of you to come," Katee said in a dispirited voice. "You doing okay?"

"Yeah we're fine," Gemma replied cheerfully. "Shall we grab some chairs and come and sit round you?"

When the three girls were all settled, Gemma started to talk.

"We didn't know what to bring you as a present so we got you this."
Gemma produced a white fluffy rabbit and a large card out of her bag.
"We thought grapes or chocolate would be a really naff gift for someone
in an Eating Disorders ward."

Katee smiled genuinely for the first time since they'd arrived.

"Yeah, the nurses love visiting time 'cause all the patients hand over any
chocolate they've got. If you look at reception, you can usually spot at
least one nurse munching away."

All three girls turned and looked over at the nurses station.

"Hey, I've spotted one!" Melissa shouted and then blushed bright red
when the others hushed her.

They all dissolved into a giggling fit and the ice was broken. When they'd
all regained their composure, Melissa spoke up.

"How have you been this week Katee? You said you were going to tell us
why you're here. Something about a heart problem?"

Katee calmly related the week's events to her two friends, starting with
her trip to the doctor's office. What was the point in lying any more?
The truth was out there. They'd be able to discover all the details if they
talked to Liz anyway so she might just as well be honest.

Gemma and Melissa listened intently to her story. They hadn't realised
quite how ill their friend had become and the concern was evident on
their faces. Katee could see that she had rendered them both speechless.

"Guys it's not that big a deal. I'm fine. Really. The doctors are just making
a fuss about nothing."

Gemma found her voice first.

"But it's not nothing Katee. I was reading this book about anorexia and it's scary stuff. You can die from it, you know? In fact, reading that book about anorexia is what showed me that I had bulimic problems myself."

"Really? Whoa! I can't tell you how amazed I was when I heard you say you were bulimic."

"It's not something I like admitting," Gemma mumbled quietly. "I didn't even want to tell Melissa and when I did, I was certain she'd think I was disgusting. I just hate myself for bingeing and then making myself sick."

"I don't think I could ever make myself sick," Katee replied thoughtfully. "I'm kind of scared of throwing up."

"Me too," said Melissa. "Guess that's why I just ended up so fat. Wibbly wobbly thunder thighs. That's me!"

Gemma and Katee both turned to Melissa.

"Oi!" Gemma said. "You shouldn't always have a go at yourself. Why does weight have to be such a big deal? Look at what the three of us have done to ourselves 'cause we all think we're not the right size. It's crazy."

The three girls looked at one other. Was Gemma right? Were they all allowing food and weight to totally dominate their lives?

"But it's not that easy. I can't eat any more," Katee said. "It's like I'm just not allowed."

"I kind of know what you mean," Gemma replied. "You see I started dieting last summer before I joined your school. Now I feel really guilty if I eat chocolate or cake. It's like I've convinced myself that they're 'bad'. Well, this is what we were all saying at the group isn't it?"

"Yeah but all food is bad for me," Katee said desperately. "What am I going to do?"

Gemma's heart went out to Katee. This was the second time she'd turned to her for help. Last time in the school sick bay, she hadn't been able to do anything but now she was determined to do all she could. She reassured Katee and then the three of them started to talk. After half an hour, they'd worked out a plan. They all realised that Katee's father was a large part of the problem so Melissa suggested family therapy. After a lot of convincing, Katee finally agreed to let Gemma visit her parents and discuss the possibility of Brian and Jane joining Katee for a family session. In the meantime, Katee was to try to be as honest as possible about her feelings with Liz and Sally.

"This is all really scary," Katee said in a quiet voice. "I'm not sure I'm ready to do it yet."

"Yeah it's scary but do you think you could try and give it a go?" Gemma queried.

"I dunno. Maybe," Katee replied. The moment she'd asked for help though, the 'voice' had begun to shout and now feelings of guilt tore through her.

"I know," Melissa suddenly said. "How about if we all do something that feels really tough? That way Katee's not the only one trying to beat her problem."

Gemma really liked that idea and thought it might take Katee's mind off her fears for a while. After another intensive discussion, both Melissa and Gemma had their own plans for the following week. Melissa was going to phone up Sally and ask if she could arrange a dietician's appointment for her. She really was desperate to start on a healthy eating plan. And

Gemma had promised that she would definitely confront her Mum that evening and finally start to talk about some of her feelings.

All the girls were amazed when Liz appeared to tell Katee that her tea would be along shortly. They couldn't believe they'd been chatting for nearly three hours.

"Where did the time go?" Gemma asked in amazement. "Would it be okay if we came back one day after school to visit again Katee?"

Katee was thrilled that her friends wanted to see her again. Although she was kept busy during the week with all kinds of therapy, she still felt very lonely.

"That'd be great," she said. "I have to know how you all get on with your tasks and I'll need your help if the docs set up a family session for me. Urgh! I'll be so scared."

Gemma and Melissa reassured Katee that they'd be back soon and would help her in any way they could. They each gave her a quick hug and then waved as they left the ward. They chatted constantly as they walked briskly to the lift area. Halfway down in the lift, Gemma gave a sudden groan and put her hand to her head.

"Omigod! I left Tim sitting in the reception area for over three hours. He's going to be so mad. I bet you he's left. There's no way he'd wait for that long. Oh Melissa I've blown it again. I've ruined the best thing that ever happened to me. What's wrong with me? I'm such a stupid idiot. I'm a total failure."

28
Learning to Trust

Gemma rushed into the lobby of the hospital and began searching frantically for Tim. Her heart sunk as she looked up and down the rows of orange plastic chairs but she couldn't see him anywhere.

"You looking for me?" A voice behind Gemma spoke suddenly.

Gemma squeaked in surprise and visibly jumped. Turning around, she saw Tim standing in front of her with a cheeky grin on his face. He was carrying several empty coffee cups and scrunched up crisp packets.

"Tim! You scared the life out of me," Gemma said sharply. The shock had caused her to momentarily forget her panic. "What you doing creeping up on me like that?"

"I'm sorry Gemmy, I just couldn't resist. You were looking around so anxiously and…er…well…I guess the kid in me took over. Sorry." Tim pretended to hang his head in shame and Gemma hit him playfully on the arm.

"Oh stop it you idiot. You know I was worried that you might have gone. I'm really sorry for being so long. The time just vanished. It was amazing. All the stuff that we talked about and…oh, we also made a pact. We've all got to do something that's really tough 'cause we managed to convince Katee to give family therapy a go. I've gotta talk to my Mum. Urgh! Can you imagine how much I'm dreading that? I have no idea what to say." Gemma was so engrossed in telling Tim the events of the afternoon that she didn't even notice Melissa join them.

"See? I told you he'd still be here," Melissa chimed in when Gemma paused long enough to catch a breath. "Though I'm not sure what he's doing carrying all that rubbish. Don't you know what a bin looks like Tim?" she said with a grin.

"Yeah you were right Melissa," Gemma replied sheepishly. "I guess I'm just used to people getting really mad and shouting if I'm ever late. My Mum's terrible like that. I was twenty minutes late meeting her at the bus stop once and she just left without me. I had no idea what to do. I felt like she just didn't care about me at all." Gemma fought back the tears that suddenly threatened and bit her lip. "Sorry. I sound all sappy and stupid don't I?"

"No!" Tim and Melissa said in unison.

"You sound like someone who's had a tough time," Tim continued. "And you really didn't have to worry about me. I was fine. The woman in the coffee kiosk is my best buddy now. She said that if I bought one more coffee, she'd give me a chocolate bar for free. Apparently I broke the record for the highest number of coffees bought in a single afternoon. That's why I kept the cups Melissa," Tim said smugly. "Evidence you see."

The two girls giggled at Tim's unusual achievement.

"Oh and I also read just about every leaflet and pamphlet in the hospital," he added.

"You did?" Gemma looked amazed and then saw the thick bundle of paper Tim was balancing under the polystyrene mugs.

"Oh yes. I now know everything there is to know about appendectomies, coronary heart by-passes and, interestingly enough, they even had a leaflet on eating disorders."

"Whoa! I'd like to see that one," Gemma said enthusiastically.

"I have it right here," Tim excitedly replied but as he tried to rescue the appropriate leaflet, his finely balanced pile of rubbish started to topple and cups and wrappers showered down all around him. "Oops," he said quietly as Melissa and Gemma started to laugh loudly.

∞∞∞

Gemma and Tim walked Melissa home before they made their way to the park. They had decided to walk around the lake while Gemma worked out exactly what she should say to her Mum. Tim was helpful and gently encouraged her to talk through all the things she needed to discuss with her Mum. After an hour of walking and talking, Gemma finally had a plan and although she was very nervous, she promised Tim she'd carry it out that night.

"Thanks Tim. I really appreciate your help. Sorry. It must be such a drag to go through all this stuff over and over again." Gemma pulled a face.

"No Gemma," Tim replied seriously. "I feel very special when you talk to me about your problems. How did you feel when Katee shared some things with you?"

"Well yeah…I guess I felt special too," Gemma said thoughtfully. "It's like she trusted me and that felt amazing."

"There you go then. That's just how I feel. And because I care so much about you, it feels even more special when you tell me things."

Gemma's heartbeat quickened and she felt a little light-headed. Tim cared about her. He really cared about her. She couldn't quite believe what she was hearing.

"I…care about you too Tim," she said nervously.

"Do you?"

"Oh yes. I really care."

"Hmmm. How much exactly?" Tim enquired coyly.

Gemma smiled shyly.

"Lots. In fact…" She blushed and came to an abrupt halt.

I love you Tim.

The words were bouncing around her head but she just couldn't say them. What if he didn't love her back? Maybe he just cared about her as a friend. It was too risky to tell him how she felt. How could anyone actually love her? Caring was different to love. You could care for a friend or a relative but that wasn't boyfriend/girlfriend love stuff.

Tim saw Gemma's expression change, as the excitement left her eyes to be replaced instead with a look of sadness.

"In fact what?" he prompted.

"Huh?" Gemma replied confused. She'd forgotten that she'd even started a sentence.

"You were halfway through saying something Gemmy."

"Oh was I? Sorry Tim. Must have lost my train of thought. Ooops!" She smiled sadly and felt a heaviness in her heart. How could she feel so good one minute and then so bad the next?

"Are you worrying about talking with your Mum?" Tim asked. "Maybe we should go back so that you can get it over with."

"Okay," Gemma said quietly. It was as if all the sparkle had faded from the day. The strangest thing of all was that she didn't really understand what had happened. It was all going so well and then a few thoughts had just pushed her down into a black pit.

They walked quietly from the park to Gemma's house. It was a twenty-minute walk and Tim made frequent comments but Gemma couldn't regain her earlier feelings of happiness and just answered him politely. When they reached the corner of Gemma's street, she turned to Tim.

"I think it's best if we say goodbye here. I know Mum. If she sees you at the gate, she'll want to come and say hello and then I'll lose all my nerve and never tell her what I've been thinking."

"Okay Gemmy, that's fine. D'you want to meet tomorrow after school? You could come down to the library and wait for me to finish work."

"Yeah. That'd be good," Gemma replied quietly.

"Right. Well then, I'll be off. Good luck with your Mum." Tim smiled and gave her a reassuring hug.

"Oh and just in case you're wondering Gemmy, I love you."

With that earth shattering statement, Tim calmly turned and walked off down the road. Gemma stared after him in total disbelief as her whole body was filled with a sudden rush of emotion. Had she heard him right? Had he really said that he loved her? She thought that she must have imagined it but deep down, Gemma knew she'd heard him correctly. And she just couldn't hide the smile that slowly spread across her face.

She walked to her front door and turned the key in the lock. Her mother's voice calling out a welcome brought her starkly back to reality and she remembered the job she had to do. Shrugging off her coat, she dropped her bag in the hall and went into the kitchen.

"Hi Mum. You got a minute? There's something I need to talk to you about…"

∞∞∞∞

Gemma awoke on Monday morning with a strange feeling. She felt certain that a lot had happened the day before but couldn't quite remember what it was. Gradually as she came to, all the events of the previous day slowly came back into focus. Tim had said he loved her and her Mum had been surprisingly easy to talk to after all. She'd expected fireworks and other explosions but they hadn't materialised. Her Mum seemed to have almost been expecting the conversation and quietly accepted what Gemma said. They had both even shed some tears when Gemma brought up the subject of her father.

Clare Williams had admitted that she'd thrown herself into her work when Matthew walked out on them. She hadn't been able to face the possibility that her controlling behaviour had actually forced him to leave. Instead, it was much easier to concentrate on her career and just paint him as the villain who'd deserted them. As Gemma had grown older though, Clare had seen aspects of Matthew's kind and carefree nature in their daughter. She'd started to feel afraid that Gemma would become like her father in other ways too and so began to push her to work harder. She knew she was being hurtful at times and hated herself for being so bossy but the anger just seemed to rise in her. All the pain and fury she'd felt when Matthew left would return and it was Gemma who received the full force of her rage.

Clare had apologised to her daughter and promised to try to be a bit gentler in future. She didn't think she'd be able to change all at once but would do her best. Gemma suggested that maybe she should consider seeing a counsellor for a while just to discuss her feelings about Matthew's departure. Clare didn't like that idea. She was certain she could cope with those feelings by herself but at least Gemma had sown the seeds of the idea. Perhaps in time her Mum would consider the possibility of some counselling.

Gemma lay in bed remembering how good it had felt to be honest with her mother. They had discussed many personal issues but instead of driving an even deeper wedge between them, it had drawn them together. As Gemma slowly showered and dressed for school, she remembered her other task for that week. She'd promised Katee that she'd go alone to the Quinn house and suggest to her parents that they consider the idea of family therapy. She wasn't looking forward to doing this. Mr. Quinn sounded a bit of a tyrant and it wouldn't be much fun if she had to confront him, but Katee was her friend and a promise was a promise. Their house was on her way to school and so she decided to drop in that morning before she lost her nerve.

∞∞∞∞

Mrs. Quinn sipped her tea thoughtfully. Gemma Williams had seemed a very nice young girl and it was lovely to see that Katee had friends but family therapy? She had immediately dismissed the idea when the doctors suggested it to her the week before. Brian would never agree to talk about their problems in front of doctors and she was certain that Katee wouldn't want it either. However, this morning she'd discovered that one of her assumptions was definitely wrong. Katee was willing to give family therapy a go and that was making Jane think. She'd promised Katee that she would help in any way she could and if that meant convincing Brian that he should go to family therapy, then that's what she'd have to do. Her hand shook slightly as she raised the mug to her lips.

∞∞∞∞

Jane Quinn knew her husband and realised that it wasn't worth discussing anything with him until he'd had his dinner and at least one can of lager. She needed him to be as relaxed as possible if she was ever going to get him to agree to the idea of family therapy.

By eight o'clock, Brian was beginning to look more content. David was out for the evening at basketball practice and she had the perfect opportunity to bring up the subject. Her stomach lurched as she tried to find the right words.

"I had a visitor today Brian."

"Did you love?" Brian replied gently. This was the old Brian that Jane had always known. She found it hard to imagine he was the same person who'd so recently hit their daughter.

"Yes. It was a school friend of Katee's. She'd been up at the hospital yesterday visiting and had a message for us from Katee."

"Oh?" A frown creased Brian's forehead giving him an intense, almost angry look. Jane paused nervously for a moment but knew she had no choice but to continue.

"Yes," she continued brightly. "Apparently Katee's willing to give family therapy a go." Before he had a chance to react, Jane pressed on. "This is a big step forward Brian. She wants us to talk as a family. All we've got to do is say yes and the doctors will set it up." In a timid voice, Jane added: "Will you go love?"

"I don't want total strangers judging me Jane. I have enough of that all day at work. I'm not going to do it in my spare time as well," Brian replied.

"But Brian, this is for Katee. For our daughter. What kind of parents are we if we turn our back on her when she needs us most? I have to tell you…I'm going even if you don't and it'll look pretty bad if her own father won't even turn up."

"Are you trying to blackmail me Jane?" Brian responded defensively. "Because it won't work. There's no way I'm having doctors telling me how to treat my own daughter."

"They're not going to be judging you or telling you how to behave Brian," Jane said, beginning to feel exasperated. "They just want to help us work together as a family. Something's gone really wrong for Katee to get this ill. You even admitted that you didn't know what was happening to us all. Now we've got a chance to find out with the help of these doctors."

"But they're total strangers," Brian repeated, in an unusually frightened voice.

"Oh Brian, for goodness sake!" Jane exclaimed. "They're not strangers, they're Katee's doctors and they know all about us already. Wouldn't you prefer to know what everyone was saying rather than being left out?"

Jane's final comment was the one that seemed to finally convince Brian.

"Okay Jane. You win," Brian said grudgingly. "I'll agree to come along but on one condition."

"Yes?" Jane replied softly. At that moment, she would have agreed to almost anything he put forward.

"If ANYONE judges me in ANY WAY then I'm out of there and your doctors won't see hide nor hair of me again at one of their stupid meetings!" Brian announced.

"Okay. I'll tell them that when I phone up to arrange our first session. Thanks love," Jane said with relief.

∞∞∞∞

Katee watched Liz walk across the ward towards her and then looked at her bedside clock.

Hmmm. It wasn't their usual time for a therapy session, which meant one of two things. Either the doctors wanted to run yet another test and she'd have to go to the clinic or Liz had some news.

"Hi Katee hon. How are you doing?"

Katee liked the affectionate terms that Liz used all the time. It made her feel wanted and cared about. Her Dad used to call her pet names when she was younger but that had all stopped in recent years. It was as if he didn't know how to talk to her any more.

"Your mum just phoned. She said that your Dad's agreed to come along to family therapy. Sally can now set up the first session. That's good news isn't it?"

"Oh," Katee said quietly. "When will the first meeting be?"

"Well it could be as soon as the end of the week if Sally has a free slot," Liz said excitedly. "There's really nothing to worry about Katee. I'll be there and so will Sally and we'll both support and look after you. Your Dad won't be able to upset you. All we want to do is gently look at what's gone wrong in your family. You're not communicating too well right now are you?"

That's the understatement of the year, Katee thought to herself. She doubted that her Dad knew how to communicate without raising his voice.

"I don't think it'll work Liz. Dad'll just walk out if someone says something he doesn't like."

"Well, according to your Mum, he has already threatened that but don't worry. We'll take this very carefully and make sure that no one makes any judgmental comments about him. He'll get used to the way the meetings work by about the third or fourth one I should think."

Liz smiled reassuringly and Katee again found herself wondering how someone could be so cheerful all of the time.

"Don't you ever get mad or grumpy Liz?" she asked spontaneously.

"Oh yeah, of course I do. I get as grouchy as the rest of the world but I try and share my problems when I do and that always helps. I have a very patient boyfriend and other friends who put up with all my moods and grumbles. Everyone needs to grump at times honey but I try not to bring my problems to work. When I'm on duty, I know that I need to give my full attention to the patients and so I try to sort out my troubles beforehand."

"Can you always solve your problems that easily?"

"Oh no," Liz quickly admitted. "Often it takes a lot of time to work through an issue or worry but the more you try, the easier it becomes. When I was going through my own eating problems, I learned how to use cognitive therapy and that still helps me."

"You had an eating disorder?" Katee asked in astonishment. Of all the people to have problems, she'd never imagined that Liz had a care in the world.

Liz stayed and chatted with Katee for an hour. Terrified of being alone, Katee kept asking questions. She didn't want to be left with just the 'voice' and it's snide comments about family therapy. Eventually though, Liz had to leave and Katee leaned back on her bed. What had she done? Why had she agreed to let Gemma talk with her parents? Like a sharp crack of thunder, the 'voice' returned.

"You're an idiot Katee Quinn! Now look what you've done. They'll make you fat! They all hate you! They just want you to be huge. You're a failure! You don't deserve to be alive! Punish yourself! Punish yourself NOW!"

Slowly, Katee started to rhythmically hit her head against the wall. She had to get rid of the 'voice'. She couldn't bear it in her head any longer. She didn't feel the pain as she continued to bang her head, slightly harder each time. She didn't see the blood from the cut above her eye or hear the emergency alarms ringing as doctors and nurses were called from all areas of the ward. She didn't even feel the arms around her, gently pulling her away from the wall and resting her back on the bed. She just had to get rid of the 'voice'.

29
Confronting the Voice

"Get it out of my head! I can't bear it any longer! Make it go away! PLEASE make it go away!" Katee screamed in desperation.

"It will go in time honey but you have to fight it. It won't just vanish and we can't just remove it. I'm sorry," Liz said sympathetically.

"But I want it out of my head NOW!" Katee repeated. "It won't leave me alone."

"Can you tell me what it's saying to you?" Liz asked softly.

"It keeps telling me how disgustingly fat I'm getting just sitting here. How everyone hates me and all they want to do is feed me until I'm huge. It tells me that it's BAD to eat. It keeps saying that I'm a failure. It's just like having a bully in my head all the time. And it tries to trick me, you know?"

"What does it do to trick you Katee?"

"It tells me that it's my best friend and that it's the only one that really cares. It says you're all lying to me and want to make me fat. It says it can make me thin and happy. I have to do what it says or else it makes me punish myself."

"Is that why you've got so many marks on your arms?" Liz gently questioned.

"It made me do them Liz," Katee quickly replied. "I didn't have any choice. It told me I was a really bad person and I deserved the pain."

"No one deserves pain," Liz said reassuringly. "Do you remember what I told you about the 'voice'?"

"I dunno," Katee shrugged. Her head ached and she felt frightened. She had needed three stitches because she'd hit her head so hard but that meant nothing compared to her other worry. All her doctors knew about the 'voice' now and they wanted her to have extensive therapy. They wanted her to stay in the hospital for a few more weeks so they could start her treatment programme.

Katee wasn't even sure any more whether it was her or the 'voice' that hated the thought of staying longer in the hospital. She'd felt a sense of relief when the doctors had taken control of her diet. She realised she wasn't able to make herself eat any longer and she needed their help. However, her greatest fear was that she'd get fat and the 'voice' just fed her terrors with its cruel words.

"Katee did you hear me?" Liz asked quietly. "I was telling you that the 'voice' only ever lies to you."

"Yeah right. Whatever," Katee said dismissively. She needed to think and she couldn't do that while Liz was talking continually. She wanted to listen to the 'voice' for a while. She had to know how angry it was. She had to know if it could help her.

"It sounds like you don't want to talk any more. Is that right Katee?"

"Yeah. I want to be left alone," Katee replied abruptly.

"I'm afraid I can't leave you at the moment honey. You've been put on a 24-hour watch because we're worried about you. We don't want you hurting yourself again. If you don't want to talk, how about just lying down and having a rest?"

Katee slid down in the bed and turned her back on Liz. She had been right when she thought that this hospital was more like a prison. Now she wasn't even allowed to spend time alone. She felt a powerful fury generating deep down inside of herself. They could put her in hospital and keep her on a constant watch but they couldn't stop her thinking. She had the 'voice' and it would keep her safe wouldn't it?

As if she'd awoken the sleeping force in her head, the 'voice' started speaking.

"You're useless! Now look what you've done! They're with you 24 hours a day. Can't you do anything right? You're a failure. A FAT failure! Why does anyone bother with you?"

"Noooooooooooooooooooooooo!" Katee screamed and put her hands to her head. Turning to Liz, she said: "Help me! Please help me. I'll work with you. I'll do what you say but I just have to get rid of this 'voice'!"

∞∞∞∞

"So Katee, are you ready for the first session?" Sally asked brightly. "Do you understand that both myself and Liz will be there for you and we won't let anyone hurt you?"

Katee nodded. She'd been dreading the family session all week and was convinced it was a big mistake. She just couldn't believe that her father would stay for longer than five minutes.

"Shall we go down to the conference room and see if they've arrived then?" Liz asked.

∞∞∞∞

Brian and Jane had already been sitting in the small conference room for five minutes. Brian had done nothing but complain since he'd woken up that morning and Jane had stopped paying any attention.

"They tell us to come here at ten and then keep us waiting," Brian ranted. "Then they sit us on these fancy sofas as though we're about to have tea with the ruddy Queen. What kind of a place is this?"

"Oh Brian, for goodness sake calm down," Katee said in exasperation. "They're trying to make it more informal so that everyone's comfortable. Stop criticising every tiny little thing. All you should be focusing on is how we can help our daughter." Jane looked fiercely at her husband. "I don't want you embarrassing me okay? OKAY Brian?"

Brian was surprised by his wife's change in temperament. She was always so mild-mannered but now she was suddenly acting like an angry lioness protecting her young. Secretly, he felt quite proud. When he'd married Jane, she'd had spirit and he was glad she hadn't lost it.

"Okay okay love. Don't get your knickers in a twist," Brian said with a grin.

"Hmmm." Jane replied steely eyed, her mouth set in a straight line. "Just make sure you behave yourself."

Jane's expression changed the moment she heard voices outside.

"I think they're coming," she whispered loudly to Brian. "Sit down and look like you're paying attention."

As Katee, Sally and Liz entered the room, Jane straightened her skirt and plastered a happy grin on her face.

"Hello Katee love. It's wonderful to see you. Oh my goodness. What have you done to your head?" Jane asked in alarm when she saw the stitches above Katee's right eye.

"Katee had a bit of an accident a few days ago Mrs. Quinn but she's doing fine now," Sally answered.

"Do you want to sit here Katee?" Liz asked, indicating a seat by her side.

Katee nodded and sat down silently. She hadn't even been able to look at her father. Her fear of him was still too strong.

Brian had noticed that his daughter hadn't acknowledged his presence and felt sad. In a quiet, gentle tone he tried to reach out to her.

"Hello Katee. I'm…erm…I'm…um…" He wanted to say he was sorry but the words just wouldn't come. "…it's good to see you again."

In a barely audible voice, Katee replied. "Hi Dad." But still she couldn't look at his face.

"Okay. Well why don't I explain what we're all doing here?" Sally announced in an authoritative voice.

Brian and Jane immediately turned and looked towards her.

"Can I just say first that we'll do anything we can to help Katee," Jane interrupted. "Won't we Brian?" she said, nudging her husband into agreement.

"That's good Jane because Katee's going to need us all to help her get through this illness," Sally replied. "Now the purpose of these meetings is to allow everyone to have a chance to talk about the way they feel. We want to try to help you interact healthily as a family. Most people find the idea of family therapy quite threatening and almost feel as though they're being judged. That's not what it's about though. We're just here to gently guide you and allow you to feel safe enough to talk, without fear of repercussions."

Sally looked around her. Jane was concentrating intently, trying to absorb every word she was hearing. Brian was looking uncomfortable, shifting in his seat and playing with an old train ticket. Katee was just staring at her feet.

"When someone has an eating disorder such an anorexia, it becomes a problem for the whole family," Sally continued. "Meal times often become battlegrounds and parents can feel as if they've lost their son or daughter. Many people think that if they can just get the sufferer to eat and gain weight, that will solve the problem but it's much more complicated than that."

For the next five minutes, Sally carefully explained some of the basic facts about anorexia. She could see that Mr. Quinn was feeling intensely awkward and she directed her next question to him alone.

"Brian, you look as though you're struggling with some of this. Is there anything you'd like to ask?"

"Well…" he started slowly. "…it just seems to me that it's a lot of fuss about nothing. I mean all teenagers go through moody or difficult stages don't they? Aren't we just making this worse by giving Katee all this attention?"

"Brian!" Jane exclaimed loudly. "Katee nearly had a heart attack. I don't think that's fussing over nothing."

"It's alright Jane," said Sally, trying to pacify her. "It's very understandable that Brian is struggling to come to terms with Katee's illness." Turning to Brian, she continued. "Unfortunately, anorexia is not just a teenage phase. Yes of course all teenagers go through moody stages. You're very right about that and letting a child behave any way they want obviously isn't the right thing to do. However, anorexia is different. Usually when a young person suffers from this illness, it's an indication that something has gone very wrong in their lives."

"Okay well I can see that," Brian conceded. "But what are you going to do to make Katee well again? Sitting around here discussing the ins and outs of her…her…eating problems…" Mr. Quinn just could not make himself say the word 'anorexia'. "…surely won't do any good."

"Talking is a huge part of our treatment programme for anorexia Mr. Quinn," Liz replied. "Katee speaks with both myself and Sally every day about her feelings and emotions. The more you can communicate as a family, the better things will be. You see Katee tries to be a mind reader and a people pleaser."

"Well I should sell her to the bloody circus then eh?" Brain laughed, trying to lighten the mood. It was all getting too much for him. He continually ran his fingers round his shirt collar and fiddled with anything within his reach.

No one else laughed though and Jane glared at her husband for the second time since the meeting began.

"When Liz said that Katee tries to be a mind reader and a people pleaser, she was talking about her personality." Sally explained carefully. "Katee tries to keep others happy all the time. She feels responsible for you all as a family. If you're unhappy then she feels it's her fault...as if she's somehow failed at her job."

"Oh my goodness! That's all my fault because I gave her too much responsibility," Jane frantically gushed. "I had to go back to work and Katee tried to help me out all the time. She made the dinner every day you know. She's such a good girl and a wonderful cook."

"It's not your fault Mum," Katee spoke up for the first time since the meeting had begun. "It's my fault. It's all my fault. I'm the one to blame and everyone hates me because of this...this stupid anorexia. I hate it and I hate me!" Without waiting to hear the reaction of her parents, Katee leapt to her feet and darted out of the room.

"Katee!" Jane cried out in an anguished voice.

"It's alright Mrs. Quinn. I'll go and see if she's okay." Liz got up and followed Katee out of the room.

Jane looked close to tears and Brian was wearing a dazed expression.

"It's not Katee's fault. It's all mine," he said quietly. "I pushed her too hard. I expected too much of her and…" in a voice that was filled with emotion "…I even hit her at times. What kind of a father am I? I'm a disgrace. She couldn't even look at me when she came into the room. I can't bear to look at myself in the mirror any more. I don't blame her for not wanting to be near me."

Jane gently placed her hand on Brian's arm. "It's alright love. You've been under a lot of pressure recently. Maybe it would help if you apologised to Katee. We all make mistakes and they can be put right, can't they doctor?"

Sally was quietly watching the scene unfold before her and she hadn't wanted to interrupt. This was what family therapy was all about - letting the feelings flow.

"Oh yes. Changes can come about," she answered. "Although you have to remember that we can only change our own behaviour. You can't force someone else to change. I think that may have been part of the problem Brian. You wanted Katee to achieve higher grades and you tried to push her into working harder than she was able to. But Katee couldn't work any harder so she just ended up feeling a failure. She also wanted to try and please you so that you'd feel happier but that didn't work either."

"So if I've got this right doc, what you're saying is…" Brian paused while he sorted his thoughts into order. "…I'm the who has to learn how to deal with my anger and no one else can do that for me. And as far as Katee's concerned, she's the only one who can make herself eat again. Me and Jane…we can't do that for her?"

"Exactly Brian. No one can force an anorexic to recover. They have to want to get better."

"Do you think Katee does want to get better though?" Jane asked timidly.

"Yes Jane. I think she does," Sally replied.

At that moment, the door opened and Katee walked in with Liz. Katee's eyes were red and her face was slightly puffy.

"I think your Dad wants to say something Katee," Sally stated, once Katee was seated again. "Brian?"

"Oh yes…um…Katee love, I wanted to just…well to just say how bad I feel…for hitting you and shouting and stuff." Brian hung his head in shame. "I don't know what comes over me. I just…I feel bad. I can't promise to make everything right for you in the future but I'll try. I get so angry sometimes and I think I took it out on you and…well…um…yes." Brian ground to a halt and stared at the floor while he waited for his daughter to accept his apology.

"You hurt me so much!" Katee shouted at her father. She was suddenly overwhelmed by a confusion of emotions and found it impossible to hold her feelings inside. "I know that everyone's expecting me to say thanks and forgive you for everything but I can't!"

Brian looked stunned by his daughter's reaction.

"I was desperate for you to love me Dad. I ached inside because you were so horrible to me and now I'm just expected to forget all that and say it's okay. Well it's not okay!" For the second time, Katee jumped up from her seat and made for the door.

"NO Katee don't leave," Sally said. "You don't have to keep running away from your feelings. It's okay to get angry. Everyone's allowed to feel upset or annoyed. You're not a bad person for shouting at your Dad and you don't have to hide from us."

Katee stopped and turned around.

"But anger's wrong isn't it? I hate getting angry. It's just not me."

"At this moment it is you Katee. Anger is in everyone and it's an emotion just like all the others. You can show happiness and you can show sadness. You can show pleasure but you can also show anger. If someone loves you, that won't change just because you shouted. Isn't that right Brian?"

Mr. Quinn looked at Sally and then at his daughter.

"I deserved everything you said to me Katee. I can't say it's easy to take. In fact it feels really lousy but maybe that shows me just how badly I've treated you. I've got no excuses. In fact I think it might be wise if I left home for a while so that you can get better without any added pressure."

Katee felt the anger start to drain from her body. "No Dad. I don't think I want you to go but it'll take me a while to trust you again. Before I saw you today, I hated you and never wanted to see you again but now I'm not so sure. I don't know. I need to think. I don't think I want you to go but I don't really know what I want yet. I know that doesn't make any sense but…" Katee's voice faded away and her thought remained unfinished.

"Katee needs to stay in the hospital for a while longer," Sally carefully informed her parents. "While she's here, we can all meet regularly twice a week and you can gradually talk everything through."

"I'd like to try that if Katee's willing," Brian said. "I know I was the one who really didn't want to come today and I can't say it's been fun but I want to give this a go. Shall we try to work out our differences Katee?"

He held his breath and looked directly at his daughter. "Shall we?"

Katee looked at her Mum and then Sally.

"Okay. I'll give it a try," she answered quietly. "But I can't make any promises."

Brian breathed an audible sigh of relief.

"Thank you for giving me another chance Katee."

Part Three
The Future

30
Six Weeks Later

Melissa looked down at the piece of paper in her hand. The appointment was for 2.30 pm and it was only 1.45 pm. She had at least half an hour to fill before she needed to make her way to the nutritionist's office. She looked at the signs around the hospital lobby, which all pointed in different directions towards every department imaginable. People milled around and Melissa paused for a moment, just absorbing the atmosphere.

Since Katee had been in hospital, she and Gemma had become regular visitors. Gradually, Melissa had grown less frightened when she walked through the hospital doors and was hit by the sharp smell of antiseptic. She had faced her fears and slowly the panic attacks had begun to fade. Melissa had even spoken about her feelings during a group meeting. She'd been amazed when at least four other people had expressed similar fears about hospitals or doctor's surgeries. The more she thought about it, the more Melissa was able to connect her panic attacks with a fear of dying.

She had realised that she was terrified something might happen to her parents and she'd be left alone. This fear seemed to go back to the time when her Mum had been diagnosed with diabetes. From that point on, Melissa had accepted that her parents wouldn't always be happy and well. She'd felt unable to talk to her parents about this in case she upset them and so had buried her worries instead. The problem was that these worries hadn't disappeared but had just festered and led to panic attacks.

"Oh, excuse me Miss." Melissa was bumped from behind by a porter and she suddenly realised she was standing in the middle of the lobby. Scurrying to the side, she looked down at her watch again. 1.48 pm. She had to find somewhere quiet to wait until her appointment. She finally decided on the hospital canteen and promised herself that she'd choose a healthy snack.

Thirty-five minutes later, Melissa was sitting outside the nutritionist's office. She was filled with a mixture of guilt and misery, and the chocolate bar lay like a lump of lead in her stomach. She'd been so excited when Sally had arranged the appointment with Kerry Walker, the dietician. For the first time in years, she had felt hopeful that she'd be able to get her eating under control. Now she felt hopeless again. The appointment was going to be a waste of time because she really was beyond help. She looked up sadly when a casually dressed young woman called out her name.

"That's me. I'm Melissa," she replied and followed the other woman into a tidy office.

"Would you like to sit down Melissa and then tell me what I can do to help you? Oh…I'm Kerry by the way."

"Thanks," Melissa said, sitting down. "I don't know if there's anything you can really do to help me 'cause I'm useless. I'm just a total failure. I can't stop myself eating all the wrong food. I hate myself for doing it but I can't help it. I've no control."

Kerry listened carefully and thought for a moment before speaking.

"Melissa, first of all you're not a failure. Many people have problems with food and it doesn't mean they're failures. It's as possible to become addicted to food as it is to alcohol or drugs but since food is an essential part of our lives, we can't just give it up altogether. However, it is possible to get control over your food intake again. That's what you'd like me to help you with is it?"

"Yes please," Melissa responded. "But I really don't think it's possible. I've tried every diet there is."

"Well, that's part of the problem Melissa. Diets usually only make things worse because you cut out all your favourite foods, which then means you crave them even more."

"That's it!" Melissa exclaimed. "I start a diet with such good intentions and it'll be going really well for a couple of days but then I get desperate for chocolate. All I can think about is eating chocolate and then it's just a matter of time before I snap and pig out." She hung her head in shame as she reached the end of the sentence.

"I can't say I blame you," Kerry replied sympathetically. "Chocolate's just about the best thing there is. I can't live without it either."

"Really? But you're thin."

"Following a healthy diet allows you to eat all the foods you like but just in the right proportions," Kerry informed her. "We can work out a plan for you that will include some chocolate but that also has all the essential vitamins and minerals you need each day. You'll find that when you start eating a healthier diet, you won't crave chocolate all the time."

"Are you sure about that?" Melissa asked doubtfully.

"Oh yes," Kerry replied. "We'll keep your hunger pangs satisfied with lots of slow release carbohydrates and you'll soon see how your cravings diminish."

"But aren't carbohydrates bad for you? Aren't they really fattening?" Melissa queried.

"Oh no," Kerry said vehemently. "In fact, when you're eating a healthy diet, carbohydrates will become a large proportion of your daily intake."

"Wow. I guess I was thinking it was just going to be cabbage stew and strained prunes from now on."

"Pooeeey!" Kerry said, screwing up her face in disgust. "You thought that's what I'd be suggesting and yet you still came to see me? Whoa! You are a brave young woman."

Melissa grinned. She already liked Kerry and for the first time, she felt a little glimmer of hope. Maybe it was possible for her to re-organise her diet so that she didn't crave food all the time.

"I want to give it a go," she announced determinedly. "I've had enough of my eating problems. I really do want a new start."

∞∞∞∞

"Are you all packed then Katee?" Liz smiled cheerily as she walked up to Katee's bed.

"Hmmm. Yeah, I think so. I'll leave my flowers behind to brighten this little corner for the next person," Katee replied, looking around her to see if she'd forgotten anything. "It feels strange leaving after such a long time. I'm excited to be going home but...sort of scared as well if that makes any sense."

"Oh it makes a lot of sense Katee," Liz agreed. "You've got used to feeling safe in here. You feel that you have no choice but to eat and that keeps the 'voice' quiet. We've been fighting alongside you and suddenly you think you're going to be alone but you won't be you know."

"I can phone you or Sally if I'm struggling, right?" Katee looked to Liz for confirmation.

"Yep, you can and also your Mum's trying really hard to learn how to help. Your Dad's not doing so great but we knew it'd be a struggle for him. Right from the start he couldn't really get his head around the idea of anorexia."

"And of course I've got Gemma and Melissa," Katee added proudly.

"You most certainly have and they're a great help because they really seem to understand."

"They're doing well themselves too. Melissa has her first dietician's appointment today you know? She's going to come up after, to see if I'm still here or not."

"What time's your Mum due then honey?" Liz asked.

"It all depends on whether her boss allows her to leave early," Katee replied.

"I see. Have you gone round and said goodbye to all the other girls yet?"

"Yeah I have. I'm gonna really miss 'em you know? It's good to be able to talk about the 'voice' and know that someone else really knows what you mean. But it'll also be nice to be around people who aren't scared by food. I like watching you nurses eat because you all seem to really enjoy your food and that's what I want to do again."

"That's good Katee. And you've been working really hard to get there but remember, anorexia doesn't disappear overnight. You're going to have setbacks and tough days for quite a while yet. You've only just started your recovery. This is the very beginning."

"I know and when I have a setback, I'll talk to someone and not go blaming myself for it." Katee carefully repeated the words she'd memorised.

"But most of all?" Liz prompted.

"But most of all I don't have to hurt myself, no matter what happens. I don't have to harm myself if I feel bad. The 'voice' is lying to me when it tells me I do."

"YES!" Liz cried out. "Brilliant!"

"It's still so hard to believe that though Liz," Katee said quietly. "I feel that I do deserve to hurt because I have got really fat. I feel like such a bad person."

"Those feelings won't disappear immediately. You've lived with them for a long time now and it'll take a while for them to slowly fade."

"Sometimes I also feel scared when I think they'll disappear though. It's like the 'voice' is my only control and I'll just get fatter and fatter if I don't have it," Katee admitted after a moment's silence.

"I understand what you're saying hon but it won't happen like that. When you reach your natural healthy weight, you'll find that you stabilise there."

"I won't just carry on getting bigger and bigger forever?"

"No Katee. You won't," Liz said calmly, trying to reassure her.

Katee heaved a sigh of relief. "I know I have to believe you Liz. It's really hard because the 'voice' tells me you're lying but I won't listen to it."

∞∞∞∞

"I'll be about ten more minutes," Tim whispered as he scurried past with a huge pile of books.

Gemma smiled and settled back in her chair. She always dropped into the library on her way home now so that she could see Tim. She couldn't quite believe how much her life had changed in the last three months. Not only did she now have two best friends and a boyfriend but she was also getting on better with her Mum.

Two weeks ago, she'd finally plucked up the courage to tell her Mum . about the bulimia. After a binge-free month, she knew it was time to share the news about her illness. Her Mum had initially been very shocked and looked at Gemma in amazement.

"You binged and then vomited a whole chocolate cake?" she'd asked in disbelief.

Gemma had carefully explained that she hadn't meant to. It had just happened. Gradually the whole story came out - about Katee and the library book which showed her that she had a problem herself. Mrs. Williams had listened intently until Gemma had finished speaking and then she dropped her own little bombshell.

"I had a problem with food myself once Gemma. I think most girls do at some stage in their life. Oh, I'm not saying they all have eating disorders but it's tough for women these days. You're expected to be perfect at everything aren't you? You have to be successful in your career and relationships, as well as be thin and attractive. It's just too much sometimes," Clare remarked bitterly.

Gemma nodded at her mother in amazement. Her Mum once had a problem with food? But she was a success at everything.

"What happened to you Mum?" she asked.

"Well I was nineteen and at University. I'd had a very happy childhood with my parents and this was my first time living alone in a big city. At first I was fine but gradually I started to feel self-conscious. All the other girls were thinner than I was and they dressed differently. I was still wearing jumpers that your Gran knitted me."

Gemma pulled a face and her mother laughed.

"Well I didn't realise they were that bad at the time. Anyway, I started to feel frumpy and out of place so I began to diet but I didn't really know anything about dieting. I'd grown up on Gran's cooking and you know what that's like. It's dumplings with everything. So I just started cutting out a bit of food here and there. Then a friend of mine suggested I try laxatives. She said they were brilliant for weight loss."

Clare heard her daughter's sharp intake of breath.

"You obviously know how dangerous they can be," she said in response.

"Yeah, we talk about it a lot at the group because some of the people there take them. It's a lie you know? Laxatives don't actually help you lose any weight at all."

"I found that out the hard way unfortunately," Clare confessed. "I did what my friend said and took half the packet after my evening meal. That night, I had the most crippling stomach cramps and spent hours in the bathroom. The next day, I couldn't even make it to my lectures."

"Oh Mum, that sounds terrible. What happened? Did you take them again?"

"No I didn't. I threw the rest of the packet away and didn't tell anyone what I'd done. It wasn't long after that when I met your father and we started going out. Because we hadn't any money, we walked everywhere and I started to lose weight naturally. No starving and no laxatives. Just a bit of healthy exercise."

"You were lucky Mum."

"Yes I was love and I can see that now. I could so easily have become obsessed with losing weight and trying to be like everyone else. It's important to be an individual. You've shown me that too Gemma."

"I have?" Gemma sounded surprised.

"Yes you have. I was trying to force you to be someone that you weren't. I was so obsessed with your grades that I didn't see you for the person you really are. It wasn't fair of me and I hope I've done a bit better recently."

"You have Mum and it feels good to be honest with you. I shouldn't have hidden my feelings away like that. It was because I was scared of you. And I also wanted you to be proud of me, you know?" Gemma admitted.

"I am proud of you Gemma and I always will be, whatever you choose to do with your life. I love you for who you are, not what you are. I made that mistake with your father. I disregarded his wonderful, caring nature and just felt angry that he wasn't achieving enough. I wanted him to be a manager even though I knew that wasn't right for him."

"I think I know what I want to do with my life Mum," Gemma said quietly.

"Oh?"

"Yeah. I really want to help people with eating problems. I've just learned so much since I've known Katee and started going to the group. It feels like the right thing for me to do."

∞∞∞∞

Tim smiled at Gemma as he staggered past with his pile of books. He couldn't quite believe how lucky he was to have her as his girlfriend. His plans had changed in the last month and he was no longer taking his round the world trip. He couldn't bear the thought of leaving Gemma for such a long period of time so it was all on hold until she could join him. He'd decided to read psychology at University, despite his father's protests and Gemma was hoping to get onto a nursing course at the same college as soon as she'd finished her GCSEs. It was all still in the planning stage but he felt excited by the way his life was going.

∞∞∞∞

Jane Quinn sighed with relief when she saw her daughter sitting on the edge of the bed with her suitcase packed beside her.

"You ready to come home love?"

"I sure am Mum but Liz wants to see you before we go. She's got some vitamin pills for me and also those fortified drinks that I still need to have."

"That's fine. I wanted to give her my new mobile number anyway, in case she ever needs to call."

"You've got a mobile phone?" Katee asked in surprise.

"Well with your father gone, I thought we should be more independent and so I'm moving us into the 21st century. We've got a new answerphone as well."

"Wow!" Katee said excitedly, before adding more quietly: "Have you heard from Dad?"

"Not since Friday love but he was fine then. He just needs some time. He's trying to come to terms with his behaviour and he really doesn't think he should be at home right now."

Brian had struggled with the family therapy sessions and on more than one occasion had actually found himself shouting at Liz, Sally or Jane. He'd managed to stop himself from shouting directly at Katee but only because the therapists had stepped in to protect her. He'd been grateful for the second chance that Katee had given him but his temper was still out of control. Sally had suggested that he attend anger management classes and start therapy himself. He needed to look at his own life and problems rather than just turning his anger onto his daughter.

After one particularly difficult family therapy session, he'd become so angry that he had to walk out. Jane was worried that he'd upset Katee when she returned home and so she talked to him. Brian decided to leave for a while and rent a flat until he felt calmer and more able to cope with being around his family. Jane was secretly relieved that he'd made this decision because she didn't want to take Katee home to the same problems as before.

∞∞∞∞

Gemma rang the doorbell.

"Do you think they'll be home yet?" Melissa asked.

"The car's in the drive and the lights are on, which is a good sign," Gemma replied.

After a moments wait, the door slowly opened and they found themselves looking straight at Katee.

"Yayyyyy!" Gemma squealed.

"Welcome home!" Melissa added as they all hugged each other.

Sitting in Katee's bedroom, Melissa told her two special friends about her appointment at the dietician.

"...and you should see the amount of food I'm allowed to eat. I couldn't believe it when we worked out my healthy eating diet. Ooops! Sorry. Not 'diet'...'plan'. Kerry specifically told me that this is a plan for life, not just some diet for a couple of weeks."

"It sounds brilliant Mel," Gemma said cheerfully. "Did the hospital give you a plan too Katee?"

"Yeah, I've got this massive diet plan. Sorry...food plan. It felt okay in the hospital but it feels really scary now. And I've still got to drink those fortified drinks. Yeuchh! They're vomit-making." As she pulled a face to indicate her disgust with the drinks, Katee realised what she'd just said.

"Oh Gemma, I didn't mean that about vomiting. I didn't want to upset you...I was just trying to..." Her voice trailed away.

Gemma patted her gently on the arm. "You silly goose. You haven't upset me. I'm sorry you have to have those drinks but it won't be for long."

"It's sort of an incentive to get back to eating normally isn't it?" Melissa asked. "They'll stop them when you're healthy again won't they?"

"Hmmm. Yeah, I guess I should see it like that," Katee replied thoughtfully. "There is something that I really want to eat again though."

"Yeah?" the other two girls said together, trying not to sound too excited.

"Chocolate," Katee said in a dreamy voice. "I used to adore that."

"I've got some in my bag," Melissa said, hurriedly adding: "But that's okay 'cause it's on my plan." After a brief pause, she casually continued. "Shall we all have some?"

Katee suddenly felt scared.

"Urgh! I don't know if I can yet," she said.

"Let's do it together then," Gemma suggested. "One chunk each. That's not going to do anyone any harm, right?"

One chunk each? Katee paused. The 'voice' didn't want her to have any. But she wanted to eat the chocolate. She wanted to be like her friends. She wanted to be normal again.

"Okay, pass me a piece Mel. I am going to have some and the 'voice' can just go choke itself," she said defiantly.

31
Two Years Later

"Did the letter come Gem?" Melissa asked anxiously.

"What letter's that Mel?" Gemma replied innocently.

"You know what letter I mean. Stop messing about and just tell me."

"What…this one maybe?" Gemma grinned as she slowly pulled a slightly crumpled envelope out of her bag.

"Eeeeeeek!" Melissa squealed. "It's finally come. What does it say Gem? Have you read it? Where's Katee? We need her here. Omigod this is so exciting!"

Gemma beamed at her flustered friend. They'd been planning their future for months now and this letter contained the final decision. She watched as Melissa rushed over to Katee and pulled her out of the lunch queue.

"So it's finally here?" Katee asked nervously as she reached Gemma. "Who's going to open it? I don't know if I can?"

"You do it Gem," Melissa said. "You're the one that filled in all the forms. Go on. You open it."

Slowly Gemma started to tug at the corners of the envelope.

"This is crazy," she murmured. "My hands are actually shaking."

Unfolding the official looking letter that was contained within, Gemma started to scan the words while the others watched breathlessly. Suddenly letting out a loud squeal Gemma grabbed her friends and started dancing around.

"We got it! We've got the flat! We're sorted for next year!"

Melissa and Katee started to shriek with their friend and the three of them hugged and danced joyfully. They had all become very close friends in the last couple of years and were certain they wanted to live together as soon as they started college. They'd spent weeks looking through brochures and catalogues, finally choosing a college which covered all the different courses they wanted to take.

Gemma still wanted to train as a nurse. Her initial desire to help eating disorder sufferers had just strengthened with every passing week that she attended the support group. Katee had chosen to do a degree in psychology. She still saw Sally Willkins once a month and had developed a real interest in human behaviour. Melissa had decided that she wanted to be a schoolteacher for children up to the age of 11. As soon as she had accepted that nursing wasn't for her, she realised that she loved looking after children. Two weeks on a working placement at a junior school had finally shown her that teaching was what she really wanted to do.

As the girl's finally calmed down and stopped their frantic jigging, a frown crossed Katee's face.

"I'm going to miss Sally you know," she muttered. "I've had so many ups and downs over the last two years. What if I get ill again? I don't know that I'll be able to cope completely alone."

"But you won't be alone," Gemma reassured her. "You'll have Mel and me and we're all gonna do this together. Hey…we'll be able to buy all our own food and cook our own meals and it'll just be so cool. Imagine just the three of us in a flat together. It's going to be excellent."

Katee smiled. Yeah it would be cool. No more family worries for a while. Now that would be a relief. She wondered momentarily how her Dad would react to her leaving home.

"I know what you mean Katee," Melissa chimed in. "It's not going to be easy for me to leave Kelly. I know that I only see her four times a year now but it's like she keeps me on track. I feel so proud that I'm down to a size 14 and it's all due to her, you know?"

"No Mel it's not," Gemma said quite firmly. "It's all due to you. You're the one who worked so hard on your diet, just like Katee worked hard on hers. I am so proud of you both." And then the excitement started to bubble inside her again and Gemma did a little hop on the spot. "I can't tell you how excited I am about this. A flat of our own and it's only ten miles away from the Uni that Tim's at. Now how cool is that?"

Katee and Melissa exchanged brief glances. Gemma had been dating Tim for over two years now and they still seemed very much in love but her two friends wondered if it would last. They'd only ever been to an all-girls school and college was going to be their first real experience of living and working around boys. Would Gemma and Tim's relationship survive these new pressures in their lives?

There were so many unanswered questions but for that moment, the three girls were ecstatically happy. They walked out of the canteen with their arms linked, talking excitedly about all the new clothes they were going to have to buy for their first year at college...

Useful Addresses

Eating Disorder Associations (Worldwide)

Eating Disorders Association
First Floor, Wensum House
103 Prince of Wales Road
Norwich NR1 1DW
Telephone Helpline: 01603 621414 (Open Mon-Fri 9.00 am – 18.30 pm)
Youth Helpline: 01603 765050 (Open Mon-Fri 16.00 to 18.30 pm)
E-mail: info@edauk.com
Website: www.edauk.com

National Association of Anorexia nervosa and Associated Disorders
(ANAD)
P O Box 7, Highland Park
IL 60035
USA
Hotline: 847-831-3438
Fax: 847-433-4632
E-mail: info@anad.org
Website: www.anad.org

British Columbia Eating Disorders Association
526 Michigan Street
Victoria, BC
Canada V8V 1S2
Tel: 250.383.2755
Fax: 250.383.5518
Website: www.preventingdisorderedeating.org

Eating Disorders Association
P O Box 80 142
Green Bay
Auckland 7
New Zealand
Tel: 09 818 9561; 09 627 8493; 09 523 3531; 09 523 1308
E-mail: anorexia@health.net.nz
Website: www.everybody.co.nz/support/eating.html

The Eating Disorders Association
53 Railway Terrace
Milton
Queensland 4064
Australia
Tel: (07) 3876 2500
For after hours help - Lifeline: 131114
Kids Helpline: 1800 551800
Parents Helpline: 1300 301 300
Website: www.uq.net.au/eda/documents/start.html

Therapy and Counselling Organisations

The Institute of Family Therapy
24-32 Stephenson Way
London NW1 2HX
Tel: 020 7391 9150
Fax: 020 7391 9169
Website: www.instituteoffamilytherapy.org.co.uk

United Kingdom Council for Psychotherapy
167-169 Great Portland Street
London W1W 5PF
Tel: 020 7436 3002
Fax: 020 7436 3013
E-mail: ukcp@psychotherapy.org.uk
Website: www.psychotherapy.org.uk

United Kingdom Register of Counsellors
P O Box 1050
Rugby
CV21 5HZ
Tel: 0870 443 5232
Fax: 0870 443 5161
E-mail: alani@bacp.co.uk or helen@bacp.co.uk
Website: www.bac.co.uk

Other Useful Organisations

Childline
Freepost 1111
London N1 0BR
Tel: 0800 1111 (Open 24 hours a day, 7 days a week)
Website: http://www.childline.org.uk

The Samaritans
Tel: 0845 790 9090 or 0114 245 6789 (help 24 hours a day)
E-mail: jo@samaritans.org
Website: www.samaritans.org.uk

Kidscape
2 Grosvenor Gardens
London
SW1W 0DH
Tel: 020 7730 3300
Fax: 020 7730 7081
Website: www.kidscape.org.uk

Victim Support (England and Wales)
Cranmer House
39 Brixton Road
London
SW9 6DZ

Supportline
Tel: 0845 30 30 900 (Low-call rate: 9.00 am - 9.00 pm weekdays, 9.00 am
to 7.00 pm weekends)
Tel: 020 7735 9166
Fax: 020 7582 5712
E-mail: contact@victimsupport.org.uk
Website: www.victimsupport.org.uk